Understanding and Using
MS-DOS®/PC DOS
The First Steps
second edition

Laura Ruff
Milwaukee Area Technical College

Mary Weitzer
Milwaukee Area Technical College

*⭐ Know difference
between internal &
External Commands*

*— where are they
— what happens to
the external.*

p. 61

West Publishing Company
St. Paul   New York   Los Angeles   San Francisco

Cover Design: Bob Anderson, Computer Arts, Inc.

COPYRIGHT © 1989 by   WEST PUBLISHING CO.
50 W. Kellogg Boulevard
P.O. Box 64526
St. Paul, MN 55164-1003

Printed in the United States of America .

96 95 94 93 92 91 90   8 7 6 5 4 3 2

Library of Congress Cataloging-in-Publication Data

Ruff, Laura B.
  Understanding and Using MS-DOS/PC DOS.

  (The Microcomputing series)
  Includes index.
  1. MS-DOS (Computer operating system). 2. PC DOS
(Computer operating system). I. Weitzer, Mary K. II. Title.
QA76.76.063R84 1985   005.4'46 85-26490
ISBN 0-314-50330-7

CONTENTS

UNIT 1 AN INTRODUCTION TO THE MICROCOMPUTER CONFIGURATION

UNIT 2 GETTING STARTED WITH DOS

UNIT 3 DISPLAYING AND PRINTING DIRECTORIES

UNIT 4 A LOOK AT MENUS AND FILES

UNIT 5 COPYING FILES ONTO A FORMATTED DISK

UNIT 6 ADDITIONAL DOS COMMANDS FOR FILE AND DISK MANAGEMENT

APPLICATION A PRACTICING DOS FILE AND DISK MANAGEMENT COMMANDS

UNIT 7 WORKING WITH SUBDIRECTORIES

APPLICATION B PRACTICING DOS FILE AND SUBDIRECTORY COMMANDS

PUBLISHER'S NOTE

This book is part of THE MICROCOMPUTING SERIES. We are proud to announce that this unique series is now entering its fourth year, and currently includes four different types of books:

1. A core concepts book, now in its second edition, teaches basic hardware and software applications concepts. This text is titled UNDERSTANDING AND USING MICRO-COMPUTERS.

2. A series on introductory level, hands-on workbooks for a wide variety of specific software packages. These provide both self-paced tutorials and complete reference guides. Each book's title begins with UNDERSTANDING AND USING . . . .

3. Several larger volumes combine DOS with three popular software packages. Two of these volumes are called UNDERSTANDING AND USING APPLICATION SOFT-WARE, while the third is titled UNDERSTANDING AND USING SHAREWARE APPLICATION SOFTWARE. These versions condense components of the individual workbooks while increasing the coverage of DOS and the integration of different application packages.

4. An advanced level of hands-on workbooks with a strong project/systems orientation. These titles all begin with DEVELOPING AND USING . . . .

Our goal has always been to provide you with maximum flexibility in meeting the changing neds of your courses through this "mix and match" approach. We remain committed to offering the widest variety of current software packages.

We now offer these books in THE MICROCOMPUTING SERIES:

Understanding and Using Microcomputers, 2nd Edition   by Steven M. Zimmerman and Leo M. Conrad

OPERATING SYSTEMS

Understanding and Using MS-DOS/PC DOS:
The First Steps, 2nd Edition
    by Laura B. Ruff and Mary K. Weitzer

Understanding and Using MS-DOS/PC DOS:
A Complete Guide
    by Cody T. Copeland and Jonathan P. Bacon

Understanding and Using MS-DOS/PC DOS 4.0
    by Jonathan P. Bacon

PROGRAMMING LANGUAGES

Understanding and Using Microsoft BASIC/IBM-PC BASIC
    by Mary L. Howard

WORD PROCESSORS

Understanding and Using DisplayWrite 4
    by Patsy H. Lund and Barbara A. Hayden

Understanding and Using Microsoft Word
    by Jonathan P. Bacon

Understanding and Using MultiMate
    by Mary K. Weitzer and Laura B. Ruff

Understanding and Using PC-Write
    by Victor P. Maiorana

Understanding and Using pfs:WRITE
    by Mary K. Weitzer and Laura B. Ruff

Understanding and Using WordPerfect
    by Patsy H. Lund and Barbara A. Hayden

Understanding and Using WordPerfect 5.0
    by Patsy H. Lund

Understanding and Using WordStar
    by Steven C. Ross

Understanding and Using WordStar 4.0
    by Patsy H. Lund and Barbara A. Hayden

SPREADSHEET PACKAGES

Understanding and Using Lotus 1-2-3
    by Steven C. Ross

Understanding and Using Lotus 1-2-3 Release 2
    by Steven C. Ross

Understanding and Using Lotus 1-2-3 Release 3
    by Steven C. Ross

Understanding and Using SuperCalc 3
    by Steven C. Ross and Judy A. Reinders

Understanding and Using SuperCalc 4
    by Judy A. Reinders and Steven C. Ross

Understanding and Using VP-Planner Plus
    by Steven C. Ross

DATABASE PACKAGES

Understanding and Using dBASE III (Including dBASE II)
    by Steven C. Ross

Understanding and Using dBASE III PLUS
    by Steven C. Ross

Understanding and Using dBASE IV
    by Steven C. Ross

Understanding and Using pfs:FILE/REPORT
    by Laura B. Ruff and Mary K. Weitzer

Understanding and Using R:BASE 5000
(Including R:BASE System V)
    by Karen L. Watterson

INTEGRATED SOFTWARE

Understanding and Using Appleworks (Including Appleworks 2.0)
  by Frank Short

Understanding and Using Educate-Ability
  by Victor P. Maiorana and Arthur A. Strunk

Understanding and Using FRAMEWORK
  by Karen L. Watterson

Developing and Using Office Applications with AppleWorks
  by M. S. Varnon

Understanding and Using pfs:First Choice
  by Seth A. Hock

Understanding and Using Symphony
  by Enzo V. Allegretti

COMBINATION VOLUMES

Understanding and Using Application Software, Volume 1:
DOS, WordStar 4.0, Lotus 1-2-3 Release 2, and dBASE III PLUS
  by Steven C. Ross, Patsy H. Lund and Barbara A. Hayden

Understanding and Using Application Software, Volume 2:
DOS, WordPerfect 4.2, Lotus 1-2-3 Release 2, and dBASE III PLUS
  by Steven C. Ross, Patsy H. Lund and Barbara A. Hayden

Understanding and Using SHAREWARE Application Software:
DOS, PC-Write, ExpressCalc, and PC-FILE
  by Victor P. Maiorana

Understanding and Using Application Software, Volume 3:
DOS, WordPerfect 4.2, VP-Planner Plus, and dBASE III PLUS
  by Steven C. Ross and Patsy H. Lund

ADVANCED BOOKS

Developing and Using Decision Support Applications
  by Steven C. Ross, Richard J. Penlesky and
  Lloyd D. Doney

Developing and Using Microcomputer Business Systems
  by Kathryn W. Huff

We are delighted by the popularity of THE MICROCOMPUTING SERIES. We appreciate your support, and look forward to your suggestions and comments. Please write to us at this address:

West Publishing Company,
College Division
50 West Kellogg Blvd.,
P.O. Box 64526, St. Paul,

ABOUT THE AUTHORS

Laura B. Ruff, C.P.A., holds the bachelor's degree in English from the University of North Carolina at chapel Hill. Her professional experience includes practice both in public accounting and industrial cost accounting.

Mary K. Weitzer, earned her bachelor of arts degree in English and business education at Mount Mary College, and her master of science in teaching business education from the University of Wisconsin, Whitewater.

PREFACE

Understanding and Using MS-DOS/PC DOS is a book written to help new users take their first steps into the microcomputer field. It assumes no prior experience on the microcomputer and is often used to help build a solid foundation for the wide variety of projects that students will work with on a microcomputer system. The "Guided Activities" approach was designed to lead the beginner step-by-step through the fundamentals of using a microcomputer regardless of the type of software that may be used for applications included in other courses or projects.

HOW IS THE BOOK ORGANIZED?

The **Understanding and Using MS-DOS/PC DOS** book can be used as a reference whenever the student uses the microcomputer. The start-up and shut-down procedures are clearly presented so that a student will have no difficulty following the steps to load any software program and to shut down at the end of a work session. A listing of the commands and their functions along with a keyboard layout is provided at the back of the book to provide a quick reference.

Background and Guided Activities When a new command and/or function is to be introduced in a guided activity, a background section will precede the section so that the student will understand the purpose and desired outcome of the guided activity and will be able to apply the technical skills learned in the guided activity to the application sections.

Since so many organizations are now using hard disk systems, the instructions in the guided activities are shown first as they should be done if using a hard disk system. If the instructions are different for a floppy-drive system, those instructions are shown in italics immediately following each of the hard disk instructions. Many of the procedures are the same for both hard and floppy drive systems so floppy instructions are only provided when different from those used on a hard disk.

Checkpoint questions are included as part of selected guided activities to help foster good work habits by forcing the student to focus on what is actually happening on the screen. Too often, students become engrossed in merely pressing keys and forget to look at the screen and think about what they are doing. Answers to the checkpoint questions are provided in Appendix A at the back of the book.

Review questions are included at the end of appropriate units in order to organize class discussion and to help the student study. Many of the questions are "problem solving" rather than "recall" types of questions. These will help the student to clarify procedures introduced in the unit.

Documentation research questions also are provided at the end of appropriate units in order to introduce the student to the original DOS documentation.

Applications sections provide an opportunity for the student to apply the skills presented through the guided activities. The student is instructed to complete a number of activities that will require logic and independent decision making in order to select and then to execute the appropriate commands to accomplish the specified tasks.

WHAT IS INCLUDED IN EACH UNIT OF THIS BOOK?

Unit 1 introduces the student to a typical microcomputer configuration and to disk care and handling.

Unit 2 introduces the concepts involved with the operating system, application software, and issuing commands. It then guides the student through correct startup and shut down procedures.

Unit 3 leads the student through some simple DOS commands (variations of the DIR command) and provides background on files and filenaming conventions that must be followed when using an MS-DOS system.

Unit 4 provides the student with an opportunity to load a program, select from a menu, and to print.

Unit 5 steps the student through some of the frequently-used DOS commands -- FORMAT, COPY (including copy commands that use the wildcard and global characters) -- and points out the importance of backups. Copyrighted software is also discussed in this unit in order to inform the new user about the legalities involved with using application software.

Unit 6 covers additional commands that most microcomputer users find essential. The student will be guided through renaming files, erasing files, checking a disk, viewing the contents of a file with the Type command, and using the Xcopy command for faster copies when using DOS version 3.2 or newer.

Unit 7 presents directories and subdirectories. These skills are presented so that the student is exposed to the skills necessary to organize a hard disk. However, the student utilizes a floppy disk rather than the hard disk to create subdirectories. In this way, students who are using floppy drive systems will have the opportunity to learn about and use directories and subdirectories; and those students using hard disk systems will not have to worry about accidentally damaging any of the files on the hard disk.

WHAT DO THE APPLICATION SECTIONS HAVE TO OFFER?

Application A is included after Unit 6 to provide the student with unguided, decision-making tasks that will review the concepts and commands presented in the first six units. This will include making use of the Format, Dir, Copy, Xcopy, Type, Rename, Checkdisk, and Delete commands. In addition, students will send output to the printer through print screens and/or the output to printer function.

Another application section is offered after Unit 7 so that the student can review the subdirectory concepts and commands (MKDIR, CHDIR, RMDIR, TREE) introduced in Unit 7 as well as some of the other commands introduced in earlier units.

These two application sections could be used as review, homework assignments, or for hands-on testing.

WHAT CHANGES HAVE BEEN MADE IN THIS EDITION?

Thanks to the helpful suggestions from reviewers and others who were using the first edition of this book, we were able to decide how best to update, clarify, and add to the book without changing its original intent. We did strive to keep the book as short as possible so that the students would have an easy-to-understand, easy-to-use, step-by-step general introduction to the microcomputer and the fundamentals of its operating system. With this type of introduction provided for all students, instructors who assign microcomputer projects as part of their courses can assume that students have already acquired a common core of knowledge about using the microcomputer. The focus can then be on the specialty applications being taught in those courses rather than on how to "boot" the system, or handle disks, or manage files, or use the printer.

The discussions about terminology, hardware, and software have been updated to reflect the changes that have occurred in the microcomputer industry. We include hard disk information and assume that many students will be using a hard disk in order to complete the assignments in the book. This does not preclude those still using floppies from easily following the procedures presented in the guided activities. Instructions for floppy systems are provided whenever those directions are different from the hard disk system's procedures. The floppy instructions are included within the guided activities and are set off with italics.

In this edition, we are still introducing the Sort command but emphasize that it should only be practiced if the student is using a hard disk system. This will help to avoid the complications that can be experienced with this command when using a write-protected DOS disk.

The Diskcopy command is discussed in a "Background" section of this book that compares it with the "Copy file-by-file" command. However, there is no guided activity practicing the Diskcopy command. The command is usually not recommended for use with hard disk systems and could cause some problems on those types of systems.

We've added the Xcopy command which can be executed if the student is using a DOS version 3.2 or newer.

As mentioned earlier, a unit has been added explaining subdirectories and how to create them, change them, and remove them. These instructions are to be followed on the student's data disk in order to safeguard the integrity of the hard disk. An application section was added immediately following the subdirectory unit in order to reinforce those skills. This unit will also allow the students to spend more time on the machine practicing common commands such as the Directory, Copy, and Delete commands.

INSTRUCTOR'S MANUAL, DATA DISK, TRANSPARENCIES

A training disk is provided along with the instructor's manual. This disk contains all of the files that are required in order to complete the **Understanding and Using MS-DOS/PC DOS** book. The instructor will also find additional hands-on activities that could be used for homework or testing activities. We've included suggestions for questions for objective testing and some procedures that may help to establish guidelines that will qualify students to use microcomputers in a lab setting. Transparencies are available that might be helpful if you are conducting a hands-on presentation of the activities in this book to a group.

ACKNOWLEDGMENTS

Our thanks for encouragement and assistance in the completion of both the first and second editions of this book must first go to the editor, Richard L. Wohl (who, we must gratefully say, never lost his sense of humor). We must also thank Connie Austin for the technical production of the book. Thanks also to Susan Smart.

As mentioned earlier in this preface, we want to thank those of you who have been using the first edition of the book and for the positive feedback you have provided. We especially want to thank the following reviewers for both editions of the book who took the time to offer many helpful, insightful suggestions and recommendations.

Second Edition:

Estelle Kochis
Suffolk County Community College

Thomas M. Krueger
Waukesha County Technological Institute

Millard L. Murray
Eastern New Mexico University

John G. Parker
Santa Barbara City College

Howard W. Pullman
Youngstown State University

Cheryl Rumler
Monroe County Community College

Althea W. Stevens
Western Wyoming College

First Edition:

Enzo V. Allegretti
Westchester Community College

David Bellin
The William Patterson College
of New Jersey

David N. Cooper
University of Connecticut

Eileen Bechtold Dlugoss
Cuyahoga Community College

Arthur Strunk
Queensborough Community College

Timothy W. Sylvester
College of DuPage

Laura B. Ruff would like also to acknowledge the assistance in this project of:
Adlophe E. Breusa and O. C. Ruff; her parents, C. L. and O. L. Blair; and her children, Julia
and Charlie. Special thanks go to her husband, Julius R. Ruff, who continues to provide
encouragement, suggestions, and backup at home.

Mary K. Weitzer would also like to acknowledge the assistance in this project of: her parents
Clara and Wilbur Klasen; and of John and Victoria Weitzer. Special thanks and love go to her
husband, Greg, and her children, Mike (thanks for some of those programs, Mike), Jim, and
Brenda, who have been patient, supportive, understanding, and independent throughout the
original and updated projects.

AN INTRODUCTION TO THE MICROCOMPUTER CONFIGURATION

SUPPLIES NEEDED

In order to complete this unit, you will need:

1. this book;
2. disk;
3. disk label.

OBJECTIVES

After completing this unit you will be able to:

1. identify the parts of a typical microcomputer configuration;
2. identify the different parts of a 5 1/4" and 3 1/2" disk;
3. demonstrate how to properly care for and handle disks;
4. distinguish between floppy disks and hard disks;
5. identify units of memory and disk storage;
6. identify the type of microcomputer configuration you are using.

ASSIGNMENTS

1. _____ Label your disk(s)
2. _____ Review Questions
3. _____ Documentation Research

A FIRST LOOK AT THE MICROCOMPUTER

New microcomputer users often approach their first encounter with the microcomputer with mixed feelings. On the one hand they are enthusiastic about discovering the many ways that the microcomputer can help to increase productivity in day-to-day applications such as word processing, records management, accounting, and so on. On the other hand, they may be a bit apprehensive. You, however, can be assured that whatever feelings you may experience, the microcomputer is an excellent productivity tool that can be used to increase your efficiency both in a working and in a learning environment.

Just as when you are learning to use any new tool, you are bound to make some mistakes when you are learning to use the microcomputer. It is through these mistakes and experimentation that you will begin to understand the logic involved in using a microcomputer. You will also discover that the machine isn't very smart and that it can only do what you tell it to do.

You won't be able to tell the microcomputer what you want it to do until you find out how to use it. A good starting point is to identify the different parts that are included in the microcomputer system. There are many different kinds of microcomputers and an even wider variety of peripherals that can enhance a system. **Peripherals** are just extra parts that can be added to the actual microcomputer. For example, a printer is considered a peripheral and so is the video display. We'll just take a few minutes to discuss a typical microcomputer configuration (all the parts that make up the complete microcomputer system with which you are working). It will then be up to you to discover how the system you are using compares with the typical system we have described.

BACKGROUND ON TYPICAL MICROCOMPUTER CONFIGURATIONS

A typical microcomputer configuration may consist of the **system unit** (CPU, disk drives, adapter cards, memory chips), a **video display**, a **keyboard**, and a **printer**. These are the parts of the system that you can see and touch--the **hardware**. See Figure 1-1.

System Unit

The **system unit** is the piece of hardware that contains the parts that will handle all the "action" that goes on while you are using the microcomputer. It contains the largest printed circuit board used in the system (sometimes this board is referred to as the **motherboard** or **system board**). Other boards and chips are added to the motherboard to provide additional capabilities for a system.

The **central processing unit (CPU)** for the microcomputer is located in the system unit. Some people may use the words "CPU" and "system unit" as if the terms mean the same thing. Technically (don't worry, we try to avoid being too technical in this book) the CPU is a chip (Figure 1-2) that looks something like a 2-1/2" long bug with lots of little legs. The "little legs" are plugged into the motherboard. This is the real heart of the system. Sometimes you may hear the CPU referred to as the "brain" of the computer but we have found that this is too intimidating for beginning microcomputer users. They may start to believe that the computer can "think" and on those rare occasions when they are feeling a bit paranoid about the microcomputer, they feel that the computer is "out to get them." This is not so. (If you start to feel this way, remind yourself that the computer cannot think; it can only follow instructions...usually instructions that you give to it.)

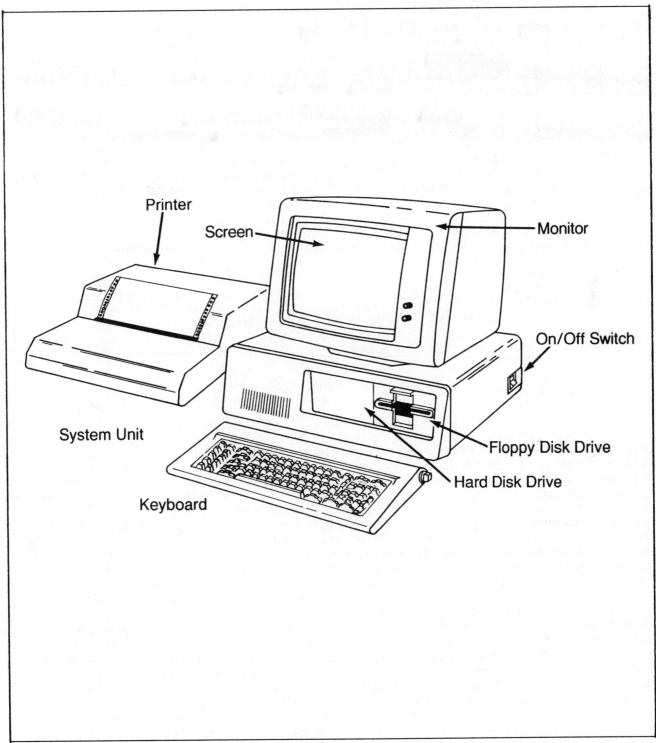

Figure 1-1 Typical Microcomputer Configuration

The instructions from programs pass through the CPU. The CPU makes sure that the instructions are executed. If the instructions contain data that need to be calculated or evaluated, the CPU uses its **arithmetic and logic unit** to perform the functions.

The CPU also has a **control unit** that supervises the functions of the machine as a whole. This unit receives instructions for the system, interprets the instructions, and then makes sure that they are carried out by the correct unit in the system.

A third unit or part of the CPU is its central storage (memory) unit. This unit manages the data and instructions so that they can be used by the other units of the CPU. For example, if there are numbers that need to be calculated, the storage unit takes care of the intermediate results until final calculation is completed. The instructions sent into the system to perform functions such as receiving **input** (data that is put into the system) from the keyboard or disks, or sending data out of the system (**output**) to the screen or printer are also managed through the CPU's storage unit. This is also the unit that is used to store a part of the operating system. (One of the main objectives of this book is to teach you how and when to use the commands to execute the most frequently-needed operating system functions.) Just imagine, all that work being accomplished on one little chip (it used to take a whole roomful of machines to do the same tasks).

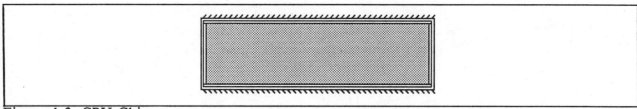

Figure 1-2, CPU Chip

Random Access Memory The **memory** for the microcomputer is also located in the system unit. You might think of random access memory as the size of the desktop on which you can work. The **program** (list of instructions) for the application you are performing -- such as word processing, electronic spreadsheet, database management -- as well as the data you are entering or with which you are working must fit in this space in order for you to be able to work on the microcomputer. Therefore, when deciding just how much memory is "enough", you must consider the requirements for the application software (programs) you plan to use on the system and the amount of data that you will need to use in the applications. If your requirements change and you need a larger "desktop," memory can usually be added to the system to accommodate those needs. Storage units that measure the amount of memory will be discussed a little later in this unit and we'll talk a little more about memory in Unit 6.

Floppy Disk Drives The disk drives are also usually part of the system unit. You may notice one or two openings for floppy disks in the system you are using. Usually these openings are in the front of the system. If there are two floppy disk drives, they may be positioned side-by-side or vertically. Some systems may have the disk drives on the side or, as in some laptops the drive will "pop-up" with the push of a button. The physical size of the drive will determine the physical size of the disk that can be used. There may be either 5-1/4" or 3-1/2" disk drive(s). The disk drives hold the disks for the software program(s) and data that you use on the microcomputer. The capacity of the disks that you can use to store your information will depend upon the type of disks that can be used in the disk drives. (We will discuss disk capacity a little later.)

Hard Disk Drives The system you are using may also have a hard disk drive. Hard disk drives are usually part of the system unit (but not always--they may be a separate unit). You may not see physical evidence of a hard disk drive in your system. It does not have a door and it does not have removable floppy disks. What it does have is tremendous storage capabilities and easy accessibility to all program instructions and data stored on the hard disk. We will discuss the capacity of a hard disk later.

Adapter Cards Adapter cards are printed circuit boards that plug into a slot on the motherboard to allow you to add more capabilities to the microcomputer system (see Figure 1-3). You may need an adapter card to add more memory to the microcomputer, and/or to use a printer, a video display, a modem, or some other peripheral device(s).

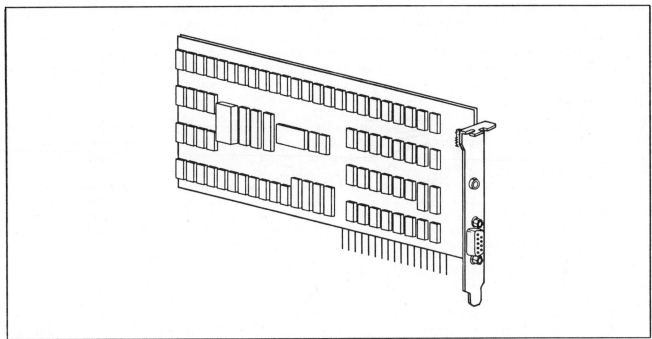

Figure 1-3, Sample Adapter Card

Video Display

The **video display** (sometimes referred to as the **monitor**) is your "window" to the microcomputer system. It allows you to see what you need to know about what is going on with your data. It does this with little dots called **pixels**. The pixels form the images on the screen. One way to determine the quality of a display is through its resolution. **Resolution** is measured and evaluated by the pixel count across and down the screen. The more pixels that are used for the display, the better the resolution. Examples of the types of ratings you may see listed for different monitors are 640 by 350 or a graphics resolution of 640 by 200.

As with most peripherals available for microcomputers, there is an extremely wide variety of displays from which to choose. You will probably hear about monochrome monitors and color monitors. Since this is only meant to be a simple and brief introduction to a microcomputer system, we will keep the discussion about displays very basic.

Monochrome Displays A monochrome display puts images on the screen in one color with another color for the background. The image may be displayed in green, white, amber, or some other "color" on a black, gray, violet, white, or some other color background. Some of the monitors have "paper-white, phosphor" screens that can be reversed from white on black to black on white and can show several shades of gray. This feature can make it possible to use software that may have been meant only for color monitors.

A monochrome display provides extremely sharp characters (better than color monitors) and excellent resolution. If you have little need for color and work only with numbers and text, a monochrome display may be the best choice for the system you use.

Color Displays A color monitor can display text and graphs using anywhere from 4 colors to 256 shades of color depending upon the monitor and adapter card used. The resolution of the color display does depend upon the type of adapter card that it uses. A CGA (color graphics adapter) offers acceptable but "grainy" resolution while the EGA (enhanced graphics adapter) will rival most monochrome displays. The VGA adapter card (video graphics array) provides better resolution than the monochrome and offers up to 256 simultaneous shades of outstanding color.

If you want to display graphs, you will probably select a color monitor. Most monochrome displays do not support graphing capabilities unless a special adapter card is purchased to provide that function. Color is supported by many word processing, database management, electronic spreadsheet, and other application software. If you like a lot of color in your life, you will enjoy being able to specify the colors you want to use with your applications.

As a beginner, you probably won't have to worry too much about the differences between displays and will only need to investigate the differences more thoroughly if you should be in a position where you have to select a display to use with a system.

Printers

A printer is attached to the system unit through a cable and an adapter card. The quality, speed, and functionality of printers varies. Your specific needs and budget will help you to determine which printer will be most appropriate. The software programs that you use for word processing, database management, electronic spreadsheets, graphing and so forth should support the special features of the printer. (If the software doesn't have the instructions -- the support -- to tell the printer how to function, then the printer simply can't work properly.)

Another criterion that you can use when selecting a printer is the quality of the output required. If you produce documents that require high-quality text output, you will want a printer that can produce "correspondence" or "letter" quality output. If you do a lot of graphs, you will want a printer that can print graphs and if you want the graphs in color, you will need a color, graphics printer. If there are budget constraints (aren't there usually?), you can find printers anywhere from $125 up to and beyond $8000.

You may never have to select a printer so it may not be that important for you to know all the types of printers that are on the market and all the criteria that you should use to select the most appropriate printer. If and when you do have to make such a decision, you will want to investigate the differences between, and the advantages and disadvantages of, the various types of dot matrix printers, inkjet printers, laser printers, and so on.

Once you have a printer to use, it is a good idea to become familiar with the manual that accompanies the printer so that you will be able to utilize all the capabilities your applications may require. You must also be aware of any special care instructions that are required to maintain the printer in order to avoid costly repairs.

Keyboard

The keyboard on a microcomputer is similar to a typewriter keyboard with the addition of some special keys. The microcomputer keyboard that you use may be referred to as the standard IBM keyboard (Figure 1-4). It has 84 keys (about 40 more than a standard typewriter). Or, you may use what is referred to as the enhanced IBM keyboard (or the AT style) that has 101 keys (Figure 1-5). Please note: you may be using an IBM compatible (clone) and the above terms could still be used to describe the type of keyboard you are using. There are many compatibles on the market that are very similar to the IBM microcomputers in that they can use the same software programs. Some have the same keyboard design or a slightly altered version.

Typematic Keys The keys on a microcomputer keyboard are typematic. If you hold a key down, the system will continue to "type" that character until you release the key. Since the keyboard is not mechanical, you will only have to use a light touch in order to activate the keys.

Keyboard Buffer The keyboard has a buffer (it "remembers" keystrokes and holds on to them until the program you are using has "caught up" to the input). Once in a while, when you are using the microcomputer, the system may be a little slower than your keystrokes. If, for example, you are to use the Return key to enter a command and the system does not immediately respond, do not press the Return key again. If you do, when the system catches up to your commands, you will have an extra Return and the system will respond to that keystroke. You may then find yourself in an unplanned location somewhere within the program or even outside of the program.

Function Keys There are ten (or twelve) function keys located either on the left side of the keyboard or at the top of some keyboards. The function keys are "programmable." For example, the F3 key can have one function when you are using the operating system (it will repeat the last command you entered) and then when you use your word processor it will have a different function (maybe it will bring up a help screen). When reference is made to one of the function keys in this book, it will be referred to as "the F1 key" or "the F3 key." When you see this type of reference, you will know that you should press one of the function keys. The functions for these keys when you are using DOS are as follows:

F1   playback last command character by character
F2   playback last command up to a specific character
F3   playback repeats entire last command
F4   skip characters in last command up to a specified character
F5   saves currently displayed line for editing and advances to next line

You will not use the function keys very often while you are using DOS in this introductory training. However, when you acquire more experience with the microcomputer, you may want

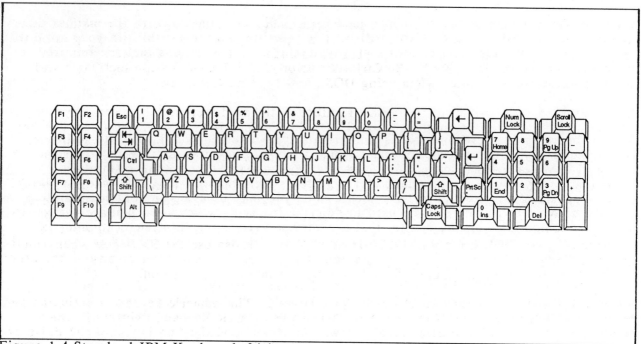

Figure 1-4 Standard IBM Keyboard, 84 keys

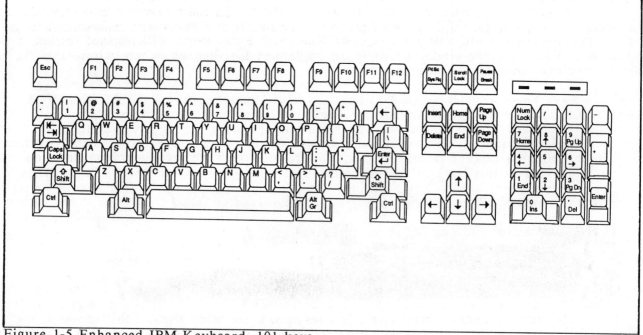

Figure 1-5 Enhanced IBM Keyboard, 101 keys

to practice the usefulness of these keys when you are working with the DOS commands. (This will all make more sense to you once you start using DOS on the microcomputer.)

Toggle Keys   Toggle keys act as on-off switches, much like a light switch. Press them once and they are turned on; press them a second time and they are turned off. Examples of the toggle keys on most IBM compatible keyboards include the NumLock key (activates and deactivates the numeric keypad), the Ctrl + PrtSc or Ctrl + P combination (activates and deactivates output to printer when using DOS), and the CapsLock key.

CapsLock Key   You will want to become familiar with the differences between a typewriter keyboard and the microcomputer keyboard. One difference is the use of the **CapsLock** key. When the SHIFT LOCK on a typewriter (comparable to the microcomputer's **CapsLock**) is activated, all keys will type the shifted character of the key. You will get uppercase alphabetic characters and the shifted symbols on the numbers (ex. shift of the number 1 is !). On the microcomputer, the only keys that are affected by the **CapsLock** are the alphabetic keys. The letters will appear as uppercase when **CapsLock** is activated. There is no need, however, to deactivate the **CapsLock** if you want to type the numbers in the top row of the keyboard. When you type the number 1, you will get the number 1. When you want the exclamation point, you must use the **Shift** key. You will also use the **Shift** key when you what to capitalize just one letter or when you want the shifted character of any of the other keys such as the colon (:), double quotes ("), question mark (?), and so on.

Numeric Keypad   The keyboard has a numeric keypad. The numeric keypad is activated and deactivated by pressing the NumLock key. When the numeric keypad is activated, the numbers are active and the directional arrows, the Home key, the End key, and the PgUp and PgDn keys cannot be used unless you hold down the Shift key while you press the arrows. Some keyboards do have a separate keypad for these keys making it much easier to use the numeric keypad to enter numbers.

Letters vs Numbers   You may have used the small letter "L" on the typewriter as a stand-in for the number "1" or the capital "O" instead of the number zero ("0"). The microcomputer is fussier about these keys than a typewriter. If you need the numbers, be sure that you use the numbers and not their alphabetic counterparts. The computer cannot calculate letters of the alphabet. It can calculate the numbers.

Conventions Used in this Book to Identify Keys

Some of the "extra" keys on some microcomputer keyboards have symbols or mnemonics rather than characters. To minimize confusion, the following conventions will be used throughout this book.

Keys that are identified by name on most keyboards will have those names spelled out in this book usually followed by the word "key." Examples include: the F1 key, the Ins key, the Home key, and the Del key.

Keys with symbols only will have the key name enclosed in angled brackets <>:

<TAB>   On some keyboards this key may have the word "Tab" printed on the key along with one arrow pointing to the left and another pointing to the right. On some other keyboards, you may only see the arrows on the tab key. You should find the tab key near the upper left corner of the keyboard.

<SHIFT>   On some keyboards these keys may have the word "Shift" printed on each of them. They may also include a hollow upward arrow. Some keyboards only have the hollow upward arrow. You should find one shift key on the left side of the keyboard and the other on the right side. Look somewhere near the bottom row. You use the shift keys in conjunction with some other key as mentioned previously. If you want to capitalize a letter or get the character that is in the shifted position of a key, you must hold down the shift key while you type the key.

<BACKSPACE>   On some keyboards this key may have the word "Backspace" printed on it. It may also have one arrow pointing to the left. Other keyboards only have the arrow pointing to the left. The key is in the top row on the right side of the keyboard. You use the backspace key to correct typing mistakes on the current line.

<CR>   The "carriage return" key is labeled as "Enter" or "Return" on some keyboards along with a bent arrow pointing to the left. Some keyboards only have the bent arrow pointing to the left. The <CR> is pressed after you type commands in order to get the system to execute the command.

<DOWN><UP>
<RIGHT>
<LEFT>   There are arrow keys on the numeric keypad that will move the cursor (a small blinking line that appears on screen to indicate where the next character will appear) in the direction that the arrow is pointing. On some keyboards, you will find that there is another keypad that has these arrow keys without anything else on them. You may not be using these arrow keys very much during this training, but you will be using them frequently with application software such as word processing, database management, and electronic spreadsheets.

<SPACE>   The spacebar is the long bar in the bottom row of the keyboard. There are some (but not too many) keyboards that label this key. This key will move the cursor to the right one space at a time. When you are using many of the application software programs, the spacebar is destructive. It will replace characters that are at the cursor's location with spaces.

BACKGROUND ON FLOPPY DISKS

Notice the illustration of a 5-1/4" and a 3-1/2" floppy disk in Figure 1-6 and Figure 1-7. The actual floppy disk is coated with magnetic media and is housed in the permanent vinyl jacket of the 5-1/4" disk or in the plastic jacket of the 3-1/2" disk. The floppy disk is magnetized so that it can act as your "electronic file cabinet" storing your data or the programs that you use for your applications.

The storage capacity of a disk cannot be determined by simply looking at the physical size of the disk. The 3-1/2" disk could very well hold more information than its bigger brother, the 5-1/4" disk. The first thing we'll do is take a look at the units of storage that are used to measure the capacity for disks (these units are also used when measuring the random access memory of a microcomputer system); then, we'll talk about how to take care of the floppy disks.

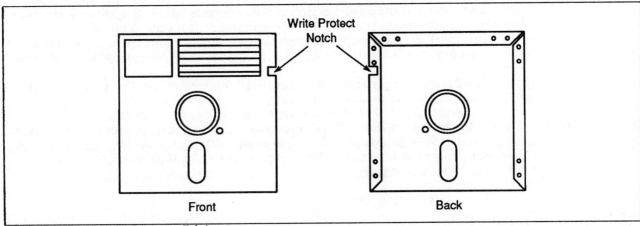

Figure 1-6, 5 1/4" Floppy Disk

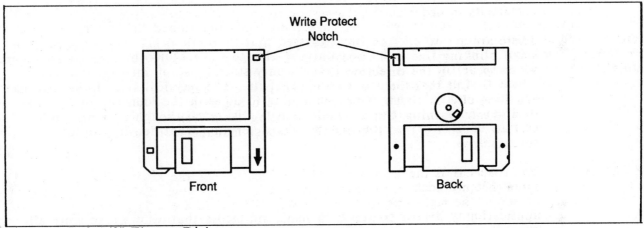

Figure 1-7, 3 1/2" Floppy Disk

Units of Measure for Storage Capacity

We hope you are beginning to realize that this book is not meant to be a technical, bits and bytes type of introduction to microcomputers. However, there is one bit of information that you should understand...one **bit** is the smallest unit that can be used by the computer. Put eight of these little bits together and you have a **byte**. Once you have a byte, you have something recognizable by mere mortals. A **byte** is equivalent to one character (like the letter "a" or the number "2"). The following list shows some units of measure based on bytes.

Capacity	What it Means:
Byte	the equivalent of one character (8 bits)
Kilobyte	1024 bytes (rounded to 1000). A disk that will hold 360 kilobytes (abbreviated as 360Kb or 360K) will be able to store 360,000 characters (technically...oops! there's that word again...it will hold 362,496 characters. Remember, 1024 x 360.) This is the equivalent of

1024 x 360

Handwritten note: use only 1000 × 360 = 360Kb or 360K

approximately 120 double-spaced, typewritten pages. From now on we'll only use the rounded version (360K) because that is typically the way that capacity is stated for microcomputer storage. You will often see this unit of measurement used to indicate the amount of random access memory available in a system. (ex. 512K of RAM or 640K of RAM)

Megabyte   1,048,576 bytes (rounded to 1 million bytes). Some floppies can hold more than one megabyte of data (for example a 1.44Mb floppy can store the equivalent of 720 double-spaced, typewritten pages). You will frequently see this unit of measure used to indicate storage capacities for hard disks (we'll talk about those a little later). (ex. 20Mb or 20M which would be equivalent to approximately 10,000 double-spaced, typewritten pages).

Gigabyte   Over one billion bytes.

Terabyte   Over one trillion bytes.

In the listing of storage capacities, you may have noticed we mentioned that a floppy could hold 1.44Mb of information. Would you have guessed that the little 3-1/2" floppy is the one we are referring to? Other 3-1/2" disks may only be able to store 720Kb but that is still more storage space than some of the 5-1/4" disks that can only store 360K of information. There are other 5-1/4" disks that can hold more than 1 megabyte. The physical size of the disk has nothing to do with its capacity, rather it has something to do with the "density" of the disk. A high-density disk can hold more than a double-density disk even though they are both 5-1/4" disks. The type of disk drive that you use will determine what density you can use with your system.

Caring for the 5-1/4" Floppy Disk

As we mentioned, the floppy disk is coated with magnetic media that allows it to store all your valuable data. This same material is susceptible to all kinds of damage. If the disk is damaged in any way, it will become either partly or completely useless. (If that happens, all the information you worked so hard to accumulate and store on that disk will be gone.) If the disk contains a program, the program will be unusable. Many software programs represent a large financial investment which must be protected. Proper disk handling will increase the life expectancy of the disk.

You will notice that not all of the 5-1/4" disk's magnetic surface is covered by its vinyl jacket. In order for the disk to be functional, certain areas of the actual disk must be exposed to the cold, cruel world. These exposed parts should always be protected. When the disk is not in use, it should be placed in its protective envelope and filed safely away in a storage device (such as a plastic diskette storage box). Figure 1-8 shows precautions regarding disk care and handling. The steps you take to protect your disks from coffee spills, fingerprints, smoke filled rooms, dust, magnetic fields, and so on will save you time and probably money in the future.

Figure 1-8, Disk Care and Handling Chart

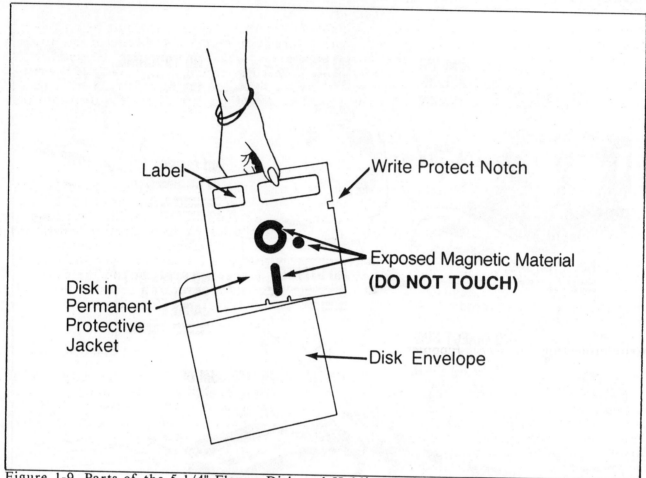

Figure 1-9, Parts of the 5-1/4" Floppy Disk and Holding Position

The drawing in Figure 1-9 shows a safe way to hold the 5-1/4" floppy disk. You can hold a disk between your thumb and your index and middle fingers. Your thumb should be on the label. Your index and middle fingers should be on the underside of the disk so that you are sort of pinching the disk between your fingers. You will also see the areas that should never be touched. Take time now to study this drawing if you are using the 5-1/4" disks so that you will be familiar with its different parts and the proper handling techniques.

The largest exposed area on the floppy disk is known as the **Head Access Slot**. This is the area that the microcomputer uses to **write to** and **read from** the disk. The disk spins around in the vinyl jacket so that different portions can be accessed by the computer through this slot. The **Index Hole** is used by the system to help locate the stored data. The large hole in the middle of the disk (which makes it look somewhat like a 45 rpm record--do you remember those) is used to position the disk in the drive (something like the spindle holding a 45 rpm record on the record player--you do remember record players, don't you?).

Write Protection for 5-1/4" Floppies

There is a write-protect notch cut out on one side of the disk. This notch must be <u>uncovered</u> on a 5-1/4" disk in order for the system to store information on the disk (write to the disk), to format the disk (you'll learn about that later), or to erase a file from the disk. If you are trying to prevent the files on the disk from being updated or erased, you should use a write-protect sticker to cover the notch. When you insert the disk into the disk drive, the write-protect notch should be on the left. This is a good guide to help you to put the disk into the drive correctly.

CARING FOR 3-1/2" FLOPPY DISKS

If you are using the 3-1/2" floppies, you are using a disk that is a bit more durable than its 5-1/4" brother. You will notice that the jacket protecting the smaller disk is made of hard plastic. You will also notice that there are no areas of exposed magnetic media. The head access slot is covered by a "silver door" that is automatically pushed open when you insert the disk into the drive. The protective door will automatically close when the disk is removed from the drive. Because of its extra protection, you might get a bit careless with the tough little disk. However, there are still many things to take precautions against and the chart in Figure 1-9 still applies. Magnetic fields are still damaging even though all areas of the magnetic media are covered. You can never be too cautious with any floppy disk.

Write-protection for 3-1/2" Floppies

The 3-1/2" disks have a square hole with a plastic tab in one corner of the disk. This type of disk is write-protected when that hole is <u>not covered</u> by the plastic tab (seems to be just the opposite of the 5-1/4" disks, doesn't it). You can write-protect one of these disks by sliding the plastic tab to uncover the hole. The tab will click in place. You remove the protection when you slide the plastic tab over the hole until it clicks and the hole is covered. Write-protection has the same effect on the 3-1/2" disk as it does on the 5-1/4" disk. You cannot write to or erase files from a protected disk.

The 3-1/2" disk can be inserted into the drive using the same procedure described for the 5-1/4" disk. The label should be up and the write-protect slot should be on the left. Most of these disks have an arrow on the plastic jacket that indicates the correct direction for inserting the disk (just be sure that the side with the protective door goes into the drive first).

BACKGROUND ON PREPARING A LABEL FOR YOUR DISK

We have been referring to the labels that are on the disk. One label is usually applied to the disk by the disk's manufacturer identifying what type of disk you have purchased (generic disks usually will not have this type of label). There is another label that is usually affixed to a disk. That label is applied by you, the user. The label can include anything you choose to write on it. The objective is to identify the contents of the disk so that you will be able to find your files when you need them.

Disk care requires that you try to prepare the label before you apply it to the disk. If, in your enthusiasm to get started, you already applied the label to the disk or the label was already applied when you bought it, you must use light pressure and a soft felt-tip marker to write on the label. If you use a pen or pencil, or apply too much pressure when you are writing on a label that is already on a disk, you could damage the disk.

When you apply the label, be sure to place it next to the manufacturer's label if there is one. Do not layer labels on a disk. The label should not extend over the edges of the disk nor should it cover the write-protect notch.

GUIDED ACTIVITY: PREPARE A LABEL FOR YOUR DISK

1. Write your name or some other form of identification on the label. (If the label is already on the disk and you have not written on it, be sure to use a felt-tip marker and a light touch when you write on the label. Obviously, you will skip the remainder of the steps in the guided activity because your label is already on the disk.)

2. Peel the backing off the label.

3. Apply the label to the disk so that the label does not extend over the edges of the disk, does not cover the write-protect notch, and is not on top of the manufacturer's label.

BACKGROUND ON HARD DISKS

A **hard disk** is like a set of giant, industrial strength floppies. It's purpose is the same as a floppy--it acts as an "electronic file cabinet" to store information. The hard disk is usually installed inside the system unit. Its magnetic media is hermetically sealed inside the hard disk drive. The disks are rigid platters and the storage capacity exceeds that of any floppy. What we now consider an "adequate" hard disk is able to store 20Mb of data (remember, that's over 10,000 pages).

The hard disk can be used to store the operating system files and application software programs used on the microcomputer system. In most organizations the hard disk is also used to store data. The program instructions and data files are more readily available and usually work faster when they are stored on a hard disk rather than on a floppy.

Hard disks aren't as readily susceptible to coffee spills and puddles of water. There isn't too much in them that can wear out...and those parts that do wear out will do so no matter what you do. However, the programs and data stored on a hard disk are vulnerable to damage. In order to learn what you can do to prevent that type of damage from turning into a total catastrophe, continue through the training in this book. You will learn how to make **backup** copies of the programs and data you store on your hard disk and on floppies.

You always want to be sure that you have an extra copy of the data just in case something goes wrong. You already know what can happen to a floppy and even though not as much can happen to a hard disk, a hard disk can sometimes lose its ability to store data on certain spots -- sooner or later you will learn a little bit about the woes involved when a disk develops **bad sectors**. When bad sectors pop up, you cannot store data in those spots on the disk and worse yet is that data already stored on those spots will be unusable (thank goodness you are going to learn how to make backups).

Please Note: This book will assume that you are either using a *floppy drive system with two floppy disk drives (one for your program disk and the other for your data disk)* or that you are using a hard disk system with access to DOS and the **Understanding and Using MS-DOS/PC DOS** training disk files on the hard disk and one floppy drive for your data disk. Be sure that you know what type of system you are using so that you can follow the correct instructions or adapt the instructions to the system you are using.

REVIEW QUESTIONS

1. What determines the storage capacity of a floppy disk?

    the type of disk and number of tracks.

2. Where should your thumb be when you handle a floppy disk?

    on the envelope - or on the label.

3. When you insert a floppy disk into the disk drive, on which side should the write-protect notch be placed?   *left*

4. If you must write on a label that is attached to a floppy disk, what precautions should you take?   *- Don't write in pencil or pen - felt pen only*
    - Be careful not write on disk in envelope.

5. When a floppy disk is not in the disk drive, what form of protection can you offer?

    to put it in its jacket.

6. Name three things that will damage a floppy disk.

    a. *fingerprints.   heat, cold*
    b. *magnets*
    c. *folding or creases*

7. Where is a hard disk usually located?

    In the system unit.

DOCUMENTATION RESEARCH

1. How many disks are shipped with the version of DOS that you use? What do each of these disks contain?

2. How does your DOS manual define the term "disk"?

3. What does the term "fixed disk" mean?

4. How many manuals are included in the DOS documentation?

5. What sections of the DOS manual would be a helpful introduction for you as a beginner?

6. What does the documentation tell you to do with the DOS program disks if you have just purchased your DOS program?

7. How can you load DOS if you are starting with a machine that is turned off?

8. What keystrokes do you use to "warm boot" or "reset" the system if the machine is already turned on?

UNIT

2

GETTING STARTED WITH DOS

SUPPLIES NEEDED

In order to complete this unit, you will need:

1. this book;
2. MS-DOS or PC DOS command program files;
3. access to the files from the **Understanding and Using MS-DOS/PC DOS** training disk.

OBJECTIVES

After completing this unit you will be able to:

1. define DOS;
2. follow correct start-up procedures including how to load DOS on a microcomputer;
3. enter the system date and time at start up;
4. change the default (logged) drive;
5. identify the DOS prompt;
6. identify the default drive;
7. define **command** as it relates to DOS;
8. use the DATE command;
9. use the TIME command;
10. follow the correct shut-down procedures on the microcomputer.

Load DOS
ctrl + Alt + Del

IMPORTANT KEYSTROKES AND COMMANDS

The important keystrokes and commands that will be introduced in this unit are:

1. Load DOS . . . . Ctrl + Alt + Del
2. Reset system date . . . . Type DATE <CR> enter date <CR>
3. Reset system time . . . . Type TIME <CR> enter time <CR>

ASSIGNMENTS

1. _____ Review Questions
2. _____ Documentation Research

BACKGROUND ON APPLICATION SOFTWARE PROGRAMS

When you use a microcomputer, chances are that you will do so in order to complete some type of a task that you have been doing using some other method. For example, you may have always typed your reports using a typewriter and now you are going to do your reports much more efficiently on a microcomputer using an application software program for word processing. The reason that you can do word processing on a microcomputer is because the **application software** tells the microcomputer how to be a word processor. The instructions on "how to be a word processor" are in the word processing program. You put those instructions into the microcomputer system by **loading** the program. While the word processing program is "loaded" you will be able to create, edit, and print whatever types of documents you may need to produce. You can then store those documents in files on your disk so that you can use them at a later date if necessary.

If you have the appropriate application software, you can do a wide variety of tasks (applications) using the microcomputer. If you have an electronic spreadsheet program you can perform calculations that you've always done on a calculator. Electronic spreadsheets can be used to figure out your budget, compute your net worth, forecast your future earning potential, or simply help you to balance your checkbook. If you have heavy-duty accounting applications to handle, you will find a variety of accounting application software programs that can do the job. Maybe you have clients' records to manage or an inventory to track...if so, take a look at database management software. Database management software will help you to analyze your data quickly and accurately.

The list of different types of application software can go on and on. Each time you "load" a different application program, you turn your microcomputer into a different type of machine -- one that will do word processing or accounting or managing records or graphing or project managing or whatever. These applications are the reasons why most people decide to learn how to use a microcomputer. This book is meant to help you build a good foundation for learning application software. That foundation begins with learning to understand and how to use another type of software program called the **disk operating system**.

BACKGROUND ON THE DISK OPERATING SYSTEM (DOS)

The name of the disk operating system (DOS) you will use with an IBM microcomputer or one of its compatibles will most likely be either MS-DOS or PC DOS. The operating system is sometimes compared to an operations manager who directs the flow of data from you to the system's hardware and then back to you again.

Even if you are using application software to do word processing or database management or any other type of application, the operating system is still in charge. Before you can use your hard disk system effectively, DOS must be installed (stored) properly on the hard disk. Before a new application program can be used, a portion of the disk operating system must be installed on the disk (either on the hard disk or on a floppy disk). If this is not done, and you are using a floppy system, the DOS disk must be loaded first and then the application software can be loaded starting at the DOS prompt. If the application software has not been properly prepared to work with the operating system, the application software cannot be used.

Many of the activities that you do on the computer will be dictated by the disk operating system. Even though it may appear that the application software is doing all of the work, often the application software is simply providing menus that overlay the real workings of the operating system. For example, if you want to make a backup copy of the files on a disk, you may just follow some menus that the application software program provides and never even realize that DOS is at work. Yet, after you make a choice from the menu, the application program will turn over the job of copying your files to the operating system .

No one purchases a microcomputer or wants to learn how to use a microcomputer simply because they want to use DOS, but a microcomputer system can't be used without it. If you understand how to use the operating system, you will be able to use the microcomputer and application software more effectively. In this book, you will learn how to load DOS and how to use some of the DOS commands that will allow you to use application software more efficiently and to manage the files that are stored on your data disk.

BACKGROUND ON LOADING DOS AND OTHER PROGRAMS

As we mentioned earlier, a **software program** is the list of instructions that tells the microcomputer what to do. You may be using DOS or one of the many application software programs that is available for the microcomputer you are using. In order to use any of these programs on the microcomputer, the program must first be **loaded**.

When a program is loaded, some or all of the program's instructions are read into the computer's memory. You may start the loading procedure either with the machine turned off or with the machine turned on. The procedures will differ only slightly.

Drive Designations

If you are using a hard-disk system, DOS and most of the application programs you will use will be stored on the hard disk. The hard disk is called drive C (Figure 2-1). If you have one floppy drive, it will be called drive A (if you have two floppy drives on a hard disk system the drives will be drive A and drive B and will usually follow the same configuration schemes and drive designations as the floppy systems that will be explained shortly).

When you turn on the hard disk system or reboot the system (we'll discuss that procedure soon), the system will look at drive A. If there is a floppy disk in drive A, the system will try to "load" a program from that disk. If there is nothing that the system can load, it will present you with an error message telling you that the disk in drive A is a "non-system disk." Make sure, therefore, that you do <u>not</u> have a disk in drive A when you turn on or reboot a hard disk system; then, when the system looks at drive A and doesn't find a disk, the system is programmed to look at drive C and continue the loading process. Once that procedure is completed, it is okay to put a disk in drive A.

If you are using a floppy-drive system, the program disk must be placed in the **default drive**. The **default drive** is the drive that the system will assume it should use unless you tell it to go to a different drive. The drive door must be closed before you start to load the program. If you forget to close the door, the system will put an error message on the screen telling you that the door is open. It should also tell you which key to press once you fix the "error" by closing the door.

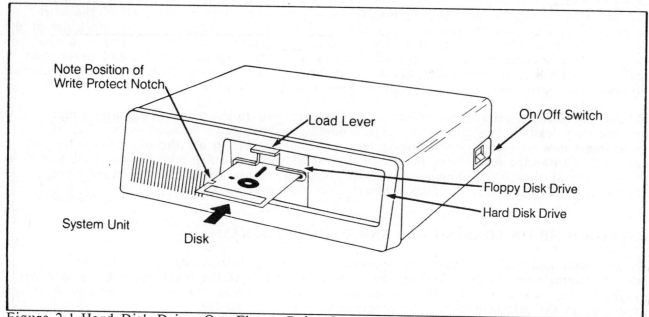

Figure 2-1 Hard Disk Drive, One Floppy Drive System

The disk drive on the left (as shown in Figure 2-2) or the drive on the top (as shown in Figure 2-3) is usually called drive A. The disk drive on the right or on the bottom of a two-drive floppy system is usually called drive B. Since drive A is usually the default drive (sometimes referred to as the logged drive), the system will automatically look at drive A when a program is being loaded. Thus, you should place the program disk in drive A when you want to load the program.

During this training we will assume that you are either using a hard disk system with one floppy drive or *a two-drive floppy system.*

If you are using a hard disk system, we will assume that DOS and the files from the **Understanding and Using MS-DOS/PC DOS** training disk are stored on drive C and that your data disk will go into drive A. Ask your instructor what procedure you should follow in order to access the files you will need to complete the guided activities and application sections in this book.

If you are using a floppy system, we will assume that the program disk will be in drive A and that the data disk will be in drive B. If your system is set up any differently, please check with your instructor about the correct procedures to follow.

BACKGROUND ON BOOTING THE SYSTEM

The term "boot" comes from a program named "bootstrap loader." This program is loaded from a chip inside the system unit and is used to start the microcomputer system. ("Bootstrap" was probably assigned as a name for this program because the system is starting itself -- the system's program is saying, "lift yourself by your own bootstrap.") When you are told to "boot the system", resist the temptation to give it a kick...what you are being told to do is to start up the system.

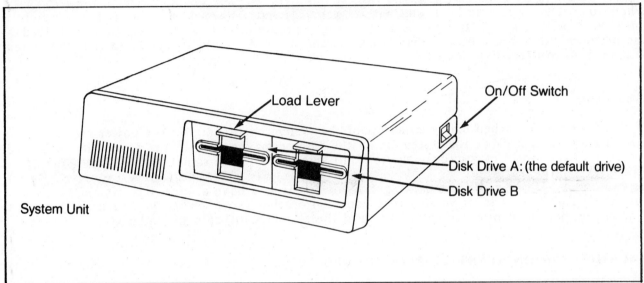

Figure 2-2 Side-by-side Floppy Disk Drive System

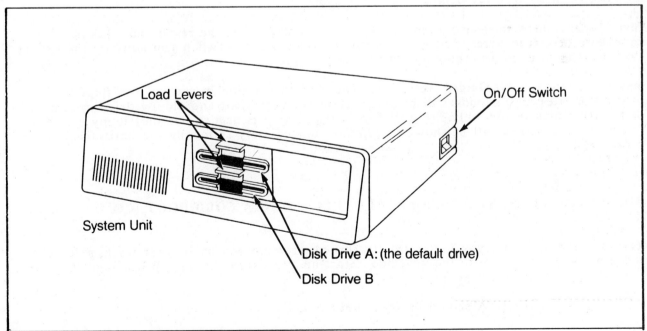

Figure 2-3 Top and Bottom Floppy Disk Drive System

Warm Boot

If the computer is already turned on, and you need to restart it for some reason -- maybe the program you are using stops working (sometimes we say the "system crashed") and you have to reset the system; or maybe you want to load a different program on the floppy system you are using -- you should press and hold the Ctrl key and the Alt key and then touch the Del key. When you release all three keys, you will have performed a **warm boot**. The red in-use light on drive A will turn on. If there is a disk with a program in drive A, the system will load the program. If you are using a hard disk system, drive A should be empty so that the system will then go to drive C to load DOS.

Cold Boot

If the computer is turned off, you may boot the system by turning on the power switch. That switch may be in back of the system or on the side or maybe even in the front (life would be too easy in the world of microcomputers if all systems were the same). If you are using a floppy system, be sure that the program disk you want to load is in drive A and that the drive door is closed before you turn on the power. If you have a hard disk system, be sure that there isn't a disk in drive A before you turn on the system. When you turn on the system, the bootstrap program takes over and the system will begin to load.

BACKGROUND ON START-UP PROCEDURES

We will now begin some guided activities that will take you step-by-step through the start-up procedures that can be followed regardless of the program that you are using. For these guided activities you will use DOS as your <u>program</u> and the **Understanding and Using MS-DOS/PC DOS** training disk as your <u>data disk</u>.

When you use these start-up procedures on a hard disk system, the results may be different from those described here. Ask your instructor what to expect when you start up the system that you will be using for the guided activities.

Important Note for All Guided Activities: The first instruction in each of the steps in all guided activities in this book will be appropriate for both hard and floppy drive systems <u>or</u> for the hard disk system only. <u>IF a different instruction</u> is needed for the floppy system for a step, the instruction will be shown in *[Italics]* immediately following the hard-disk procedure.

GUIDED ACTIVITY: START-UP PROCEDURES USING A COLD BOOT (COMPUTER IS OFF WHEN YOU START)

NOTE: If the computer you use is usually turned on when you begin your work, skip this guided activity and go on to the next one, "Start-up Procedures Using a Warm Boot (Computer is On When You Start)", page 26.

1. The door on drive A should be open and the drive should be empty.

If you are using a hard disk, you should now skip to step 5. Steps 2 through 4 explain how to insert the DOS program disk into the drive on a floppy system. You don't have to do this on a hard disk because the DOS programs are already stored on the hard disk.

2.   *[If you are using a floppy disk system: Carefully remove the DOS disk from the paper envelope.*

Notice that the exposed areas of the disk are now unprotected. Never touch the exposed magnetic material. The side of the disk with the two small cut out notches should be inserted into the drive first. You want to practice a "thumbs up" policy when you insert the program disk carefully into disk drive A. In other words, there is only one correct way to insert the disk into the drive. You should be holding the disk as described here and on page 14. Your thumb should be on the label and facing the ceiling when you slide the disk into the drive. The write-protect notch should be on the left. If you put the disk in any other way, the system will give you an error message. (If this should happen, you simply remove the disk and try again.) Figure 2-4 illustrates correct disk insertion.

3.   *Gently slide the disk straight into the drive. Do not bend the disk. If there is any resistance, do not force the disk. (If necessary, slide the disk out and try again.)*

4.   *When the disk is fully inserted, close the drive door. (There may be a turn-button instead of an actual door that is used to "close" the drive.) Continue with step 5.]*

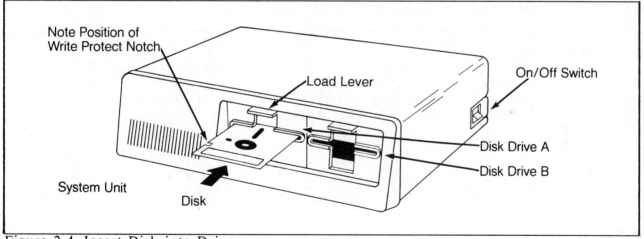

Figure 2-4, Insert Disk into Drive

5.   If you are using a system with a printer, check to be sure that the printer is turned on and online.

6.   Locate the power switch and turn on the system.

The system may make some whirring sounds as it warms up and begins to check itself out (it has to make sure that it feels like going to work). When it decides that it feels okay, it looks at drive A. The red in-use light will come on. Whenever a red in-use light is on, do not open the drive door. The light means that the system is trying to get information from the disk (reading the disk) or storing information on the disk (writing to the disk) in that drive. If you interrupt this process by opening the drive door, you may damage the drive and/or the disk.

If there is a disk in drive A, the system will attempt to load the part of the DOS program that it needs in order to continue any other operations. If there is no disk in drive A and you are using a hard disk system, the system will then look at drive C (remember, that's the hard disk). It will then find the part of DOS that it needs to continue. If there is a disk in drive A, the system will try to find the part of DOS that it needs on that disk. If DOS can't be found, you will receive an error message. You must then either replace the floppy disk with one that does have DOS (if you are using a floppy system) or remove the disk from drive A (if you are using a hard disk system).

[Note for floppy disk systems: the **Understanding and Using MS-DOS/PC DOS** *training disk does have part of DOS on it but do* not *put that disk in drive A for this activity. The DOS disk should be in drive A.]*

The system may now be displaying a message asking you for the date (Figure 2-5). Some systems do not stop to ask for the date because there is an internal clock that will automatically keep track of the current date and time.

7. Adjust the contrast and brightness controls on the monitor so that the image is at a comfortable level.

8. End of this guided activity. Continue on to the next section.

BACKGROUND ON CURSOR

Notice the little blinking line next to the request for the date (or elsewhere on the screen depending upon how the system has been set up). That is a **cursor**. The **cursor** indicates where the next character will appear on the screen.

```
          Current date is Tue 1-01-1980
          Enter new Date: __
```

Figure 2-5, Sample DOS Request for Date

GUIDED ACTIVITY: START-UP PROCEDURES USING A WARM BOOT (COMPUTER IS ON WHEN YOU START)

You are now going to warm boot the system that you are using. Remember, a warm boot is performed on a system that is already turned on.

1. The door on drive A should be open and the drive should be empty, *(unless you are using a floppy system and the DOS disk is still in the drive from the previous guided activity. In that case leave it there and continue on to step 5 in this guided activity.)*

If you are using a hard disk, you should now skip to step 5. Steps 2 through 4 explain how to insert the DOS program disk into the drive on a floppy system. You don't have to do this on a hard disk because the DOS programs are already stored on the hard disk.

2.   *[If you are using a floppy disk system: Carefully remove the DOS disk from the paper envelope.*

Notice that the exposed areas of the disk are now unprotected. Never touch the exposed magnetic material. The side of the disk with the two small cut out notches should be inserted into the drive first. You want to practice a "thumbs up" policy when you insert the program disk carefully into disk drive A. In other words, there is only one correct way to insert the disk into the drive. You should be holding the disk as described here and on page 14. Your thumb should be on the label and facing the ceiling when you slide the disk into the drive. The write-protect notch should be on the left. If you put the disk in any other way, the system will give you an error message. (If this should happen, you simply remove the disk and try again.) Figure 2-4 illustrates correct disk insertion.

3.   *Gently slide the disk straight into the drive. Do not bend the disk. If there is any resistance, do not force the disk. (If necessary, slide the disk out and try again.)*

4.   *When the disk is fully inserted, close the drive door. (There may be a turn-button instead of an actual door that is used to "close" the drive.) Continue with step 5.]*

5.   Load DOS by pressing and holding the **Ctrl key** and the **Alt key**. Then, press the **Del key**. RELEASE ALL THREE KEYS.

The red in-use light will come on (this may not be visible on the hard disk you are using). Whenever the red in-use light is on a floppy drive, do not open the drive door. The light means that the system is trying to get information from the disk (reading the disk) or storing information on the disk (writing to the disk) in that drive. If you interrupt this process by opening the drive door, you may damage the drive and/or the disk.

If there is a disk in drive A, the system will attempt to load the part of the DOS program that it needs in order to continue any other operations. If there isn't any disk in drive A and you are using a hard disk system, the system will then look at drive C (remember, that's the hard disk). It will then find the part of DOS that it needs to continue. If there is a disk in drive A, the system will try to find the part of DOS that it needs on that disk. If DOS can't be found, you will receive an error message. You must then either replace the floppy disk with one that does have DOS (if you are using a floppy system) or remove the disk from drive A (if you are using a hard disk system).

*[Note for floppy disk systems: the **Understanding and Using MS-DOS/PC DOS** training disk does have part of DOS on it but do not put that disk in drive A for this activity. The DOS disk should be in drive A.]*

The system may now be displaying a message asking you for the date (Figure 2-5). Some systems do not stop to ask for the date because there is an internal clock that will automatically keep track of the current date and time.

6.   Use the procedures explained in steps 2 through 4 to insert the **Understanding and Using MS-DOS/PC DOS** training disk into the data disk drive. (That's drive A on a hard disk system or *[drive B on a floppy drive system]*.)

7.   End of this guided activity. Continue on to the next section.

BACKGROUND ON ENTERING THE DATE AND TIME

It is strongly recommended that you allow the system to "time stamp" the files you are using by entering the correct date and time whenever you begin a work session. It is possible to bypass the request for the date and time by pressing the Return key twice. However, when you bypass the request, the current date and time are not valid and you forego a valuable DOS function. By time stamping the files, you will have a record of when a file was created or when you edited it last. You may also be able to take advantage of the system's date and time through some of the functions available in the application software you use. (Some microcomputers may have an internal clock that automatically maintains the correct date and time. If your system has this feature, you may skip these procedures.)

GUIDED ACTIVITY: ENTER THE DATE AND TIME

As shown in Figure 2-5, the system may be asking you to enter today's date.

1.   Type the current date in the following format: **mm/dd/yy** or **mm-dd-yy**

For example, if the date is January 30, 1991, you will type **1/30/91** or **1-30-91**. Do not type in the name of the day. This will result in an "invalid date" message. Important: Type the numbers using the top row of numbers on the keyboard. Never use the letter "O" for the zero or the letter "l" for the number one. The microcomputer system will not read these characters as numbers and this can cause you problems both when you are using DOS as well as when you are using application software.

2.   Press **<CR>**

If you use the wrong format when you type the date, the system will prompt "Invalid Date" and give you a chance to enter the date again. If this happens, simply retype the date using the format described previously. Be careful not to enter any spaces in the date. If you entered the date correctly, the system will now be requesting the time (Figure 2-6). Let's not keep it waiting.

```
Current time is 0:00:30.04
Enter new time:__
```

Figure 2-6, Sample DOS Request for Time

3.   Type the current time using this format: **xx:xx**

Fill in the appropriate numbers where x's appear using 24-hour time to distinguish a.m. from p.m. Do not type "a.m." or "p.m." (For example, 10:15 a.m. is simply typed as **10:15** -- no other time indicators are required. If you are starting at 1:15 in the afternoon, type **13:15**) Be sure to hold down <SHIFT> when you type the colon between the hour and minutes.

4.   Press **<CR>**

If you use an incorrect format when you type the time, the system will prompt "Invalid time" and give you a chance to enter the time again. If this happens, retype the time using the format described previously. Be careful not to enter any spaces in the time and be sure to use the colon between the hour and minutes rather than the semicolon.

If you enter the time correctly, the DOS prompt will appear on the screen.

If you are using a hard disk system, you might have the **C>**_ prompt on the screen or if your system is set up differently you might have some type of menu on the screen. (If you are using a hard disk system and you have anything other than the **C>**_ prompt on the screen, check with your instructor to find out what procedures you should use in order to access the files you will need during this training.)

[If you are using a floppy system, the DOS prompt will appear as A>__ with the cursor blinking next to it.]

5.   End of this guided activity. Continue on to the next section.

BACKGROUND ON THE DOS PROMPT AND CHANGING THE DEFAULT (LOGGED) DRIVE

The DOS prompt should be on the screen. If you are using a standard two-drive floppy drive system, the prompt probably appears as **A>**_. This prompt lets you know that the default drive is drive A. If the prompt is **C>**_, that indicates that drive C is the default drive. Remember, the system will automatically go to the disk in the default drive unless you specify that it should go to a different drive.

If you are planning to perform a number of operations on the files in a drive that is not the default, you may wish to change the default disk drive. This change can be made by typing the letter of the drive you wish to designate as the default followed by a colon. When you press <CR> the DOS prompt will indicate the letter of the new default drive. When you reload the system the former default will be reactivated; or if you type a new default drive designation, the default will change.

BACKGROUND ON ISSUING AND CORRECTING DOS COMMANDS

You will notice that the cursor is blinking next to the DOS prompt. If the DOS prompt is the last thing on the screen and the cursor is blinking right next to it, you will know which drive is the default drive and that DOS is waiting for your next command.

A **command** is an instruction that you issue to the system telling it to perform a function. Throughout the remainder of this training, you will be issuing several different commands using terms that DOS can understand. There are a few guidelines that will help to make you more successful with DOS.

Case When you type the commands, the spacing and use of colons in appropriate places will be extremely important. The characters used, however, can be typed in all uppercase or all lowercase or a combination of both. DOS isn't fussy about the case used. In this book, we are showing all commands in uppercase so that they will be easier for you to read.

Correcting a Typing Mistake If you make a mistake as you are typing a command and you haven't pressed <CR> yet, you can use <BACKSPACE> to erase one character at a time to the left of the cursor's location. If the command is totally messed up (it could happen), you could press the Esc key. A backslash (\) will appear on the line and the cursor will go to the next line so that you can type the command again. Don't worry about anything on the screen above the cursor. You can't go back to change it and the system doesn't care about it. If you are a perfectionist and there are some old mistakes on the screen that are bothering you, you will learn how to clear the screen a little later in the training.

Entering the Command When you finish typing a command, press <CR> to get the system to accept the command and to begin the function you requested through the command.

Bad Command or Filename (or other error messages) Once you execute the command by pressing the Return key, you may get unexpected results. If this should happen, just check to be sure that you have typed the command correctly. If you notice that a mistake was made, retype the command at the current DOS prompt.

Stop a Command in Progress If a command is executing and you want to stop it, you can press and hold the Ctrl key and then touch the Break key (usually the same key as the ScrollLock key located somewhere on the top row of the keyboard). Execution of the command will stop and the system prompt will reappear. You can then type your next command.

GUIDED ACTIVITY: CHANGING THE DEFAULT (LOGGED) DRIVE

The cursor should appear to the right of the DOS prompt. The DOS prompt (C> or A>) should be on the screen indicating the default drive. You are going to change the default drive.

1.   Type A:

     [*If you are using a floppy drive system type B:*]   B: enter

2.   Press **<CR>**

     Notice the DOS prompt now indicates the new default drive (either A> or B> depending upon the system you are using). This book assumes that the default drive on a hard disk system is drive C and that *the default drive on a floppy disk system is drive A.* You will now change the default drive back to what it was when you started.

3.   Type C: NO

     [*If you are using a floppy drive system type A:*]   A: enter

4.   Press **<CR>**

Notice that the DOS prompt once again indicates the starting default drive (C> on a hard disk system and *A> on a floppy disk drive system.*)

5.   End of this guided activity. Continue on to the next section.

BACKGROUND ON RESETTING THE DOS DATE AND TIME

If you entered the wrong date or the wrong time when you booted the system, there are two DOS commands (creatively called "Date" and "Time") that can be used to rectify the error.

Please note that these commands can be used if your system has a built-in clock and the date and/or time it set is incorrect (maybe it's leap year or maybe there was a time change to or from daylight-saving time), however, the time correction will only be effective during the current work session. The next time you reboot the system, the incorrect date and/or time will reappear. The only way to fix the built-in clock is to use the "clock" command that is written for your system -- you will have to check the documentation to find out exactly what command will work on your system. Look for something like RTCLOCK.COM or ASTCLOCK.COM.

GUIDED ACTIVITY: RESET THE SYSTEM DATE AND TIME

The DOS prompt should be on the screen with the cursor next to it.

1.   Type **DATE**

2.   Press **<CR>**

    The "Current date is... Enter new date:" message will appear.

3.   Type the correct date using the same procedures you used when you started the system (p. 28) and then press **<CR>**.

    If you discover that the date was indeed entered correctly, just press **<CR>** to indicate that it is the correct date. The DOS prompt will be the last thing on the screen.

4.   Type **TIME**

5.   Press **<CR>**

    The "Current time is... Enter new time:" message will appear.

6.   Type the correct time using the same procedures you used when you started the system (p. 28) and then press **<CR>**

    If you discover that the time was indeed entered correctly, just press **<CR>** to indicate that it is the correct time. The DOS prompt will be the last thing on the screen.

7.   End of this guided activity. Continue on to the next section.

BACKGROUND ON SHUT-DOWN PROCEDURES

When you are finished with a work session at the microcomputer, you want to be sure to follow appropriate shut-down procedures, primarily to avoid losing data. Each software program that you use will have a specific shut-down routine. It may require that a certain menu be on the screen before you remove the disks from the drives or it may require that you exit out of the program so that a system menu or the DOS prompt is on the screen. Still others may have no specifications at all.

It is always a good idea to find out what exit or shut-down procedures are required with each new software package that you use. When you are using DOS, probably the safest procedure is to be sure that the DOS prompt is the last thing on the screen and that the cursor is blinking just to the right of the prompt. We will take a moment now to practice some shut-down procedures.

GUIDED ACTIVITY: SHUT-DOWN PROCEDURES

1. Make sure that you have followed the proper escape or exit procedures that may be recommended for the software you are using. Failure to follow such precautions may result in lost data.

   Since you are using DOS, you are at a safe place to stop if the DOS prompt (C> or A>) is the last thing on the screen and the cursor is next to it.

2. Be sure that the red in-use disk drive lights are off for the drives.

3. Carefully open a disk drive door and remove the floppy disk from the drive. Do not close the drive door. (On a two-drive system, it really doesn't matter which disk you remove first.)

   When there is no disk in the floppy disk drive, it is better to leave the door open in order to avoid putting too much pressure on the read-write heads.

4. Put the disk into its protective envelope.

   It is a good idea to have the protective envelope readily available when you remove a disk from the drive so that you can put the disk into protective custody as soon as it is removed. Don't even put it on the table for a brief moment. You might put it on a dusty area, or in something that had been spilled, or maybe someone will come over to talk with you and rest their hand on your exposed disk. Danger is lurking everywhere. The old saying, "better safe than sorry", certainly applies when handling floppy disks. It's no fun trying to replace lost data. (If you are using one of the 3-1/2" disks, you might not have an envelope because they have the extra protection that we discussed earlier.)

5. If you have another floppy disk, use the same procedure discussed in steps 3 and 4 to remove it.

6. At this point in the shut-down procedures, follow the steps suggested by your organization. Some places do not turn the power off on the microcomputer but simply turn the contrast down on the display to avoid the possibility of shadows being burned into the display. Other places leave the machines on but would prefer that the display

buttons be left alone. Or, possibly you will be asked to turn off the machines. It is best to check if you are unsure of your organization's policy.

7. Last guided activity in this unit.

DOS prompt - A:>

REVIEW QUESTIONS

1. How do you load DOS?

   turn on

2. When the disk drive in-use light is on, is it safe to open the drive door?

   no

3. When you insert the DOS disk into drive A on a floppy disk system and close the door, is DOS loaded? *yes*

4. Assume that today's date is January 15, 1991. Write the date exactly as you would type it when you start up the microcomputer system.

   01:15:91

5. Which key do you press to get the system to accept the date that you type when you start the system?

   enter

6. If you receive an "invalid date" message, what should you do?

   backup and retype

7. If it is 2 p.m., how will you enter the time?

   14:00

8. If you receive an "invalid time" message, what should you do?

   backup and retype

9. Illustrate how the DOS prompt looks on the screen of the system you use? What does the DOS prompt indicate?

   A:> = system is ready.

10. Which key should you press to get the system to execute a command?

    cursor CR or enter

11. If you receive a "bad command or filename" message, what should you do?

    retype the command

12. Drive C is the default drive, what should you type to change the default to drive A?

    A: press CR   Read unit 3 →

DOCUMENTATION RESEARCH

1. What happens when you load DOS?

2. Does your system have a built-in clock? If "yes", what command will allow you to set the date and time for the clock?

3. What keystrokes do you use to print what is on the screen?

4. What keystrokes do you use to send output to the printer as well as to the screen?

5. What keystrokes do you use to turn off the output to printer.

6. How does the DOS documentation define "file"?

7. If you have several files on a disk in drive A, and you are only interested in displaying the name of one of the files, MYFILE.BAS, write the command you would use.

8. If you want to print a directory from the disk in drive A but not display it on the screen, what command would you type?

NOTES:

UNIT
3
DISPLAYING AND PRINTING DIRECTORIES

SUPPLIES NEEDED

In order to complete this unit, you will need:

1. this book;
2. DOS command program files;
3. the **Understanding and Using MS-DOS/PC DOS** training disk.

OBJECTIVES

After completing this unit you will be able to:

1. define **file**;
2. display a full directory of a disk;
3. display a full directory that will pause before scrolling off screen;
4. identify parameters for file specifications;
5. display a wide directory of a disk;
6. display a sorted directory;
7. clear the screen;
8. generate output to printer;
9. stop output to printer.

no pause
DIR A: then
DIR B: <CR>

a pause
DIR B: /P
then <CR>

IMPORTANT KEYSTROKES AND COMMANDS

The important keystrokes and commands that will be introduced in this unit are:

1. Display a full directory (no pause) .... DIR or DIR A: or DIR B:
   then <CR>
2. Display a full directory with a pause .... DIR /P or DIR A: /P or DIR B: /P
   then <CR>

3. Display a wide directory . . . . DIR /W or DIR A: /W or DIR B: /W
4. Display a sorted directory . . . . DIR A: ¦ SORT or DIR B: ¦ SORT
5. Display a directory listing specific filename . . . . DIR A:filename.ext or
                                                                       DIR B:filename.ext
6. Print the screen . . . . <SHIFT> + PrtSc or on some systems
                                                                       Print Screen key
7. Output to printer . . . . Ctrl + PrtSc or Ctrl + P
8. Clear the screen . . . . CLS <CR>

ASSIGNMENTS

1. _____ Print Screen Function
2. _____ Output to Printer Function
3. _____ Review Questions
4. _____ Documentation Research

BACKGROUND ON FILES

You will be doing a **directory** that will list all the names of the files that are stored on a disk. All information with which the computer works is stored in **files**. Any program disk with which you may be working consists of various programs contained in files. Anything that you create on a computer can be stored in a file on a disk, for example, a graph, a word processing document, a database, or a spreadsheet. One definition that you might use for a **file** is simply that it is a related group of data stored on a disk and given a filename.

BACKGROUND ON FILENAME PARAMETERS

The operating system has very specific and rigid rules for naming files. The filename itself can have from one to eight characters. In addition to the actual filename, an optional extension of from one to three characters can be assigned to a filename. A filename and its extension are separated by a period.

Once a filename has been given an extension, the use of the extension is no longer optional. Ordinarily, it must be included with the filename whenever reference is made to that file. Sometimes you cannot add your own filename extensions because some application programs will do so automatically.

The only valid characters for filenames and the optional extensions are:

A through Z 0 through 9 $ & @ % _ - ( ) ' ' { } # !
no spaces

The rules for naming files are dictated by the operating system and are in force when you are using application software. Once you learn the rules for naming files for the operating system, you don't have to learn all new rules for the application software you are using. Some application software may be more restrictive with the characters allowed in filenames. The majority of them seem to permit A through Z and 0 through 9 and the underscore character.

Parameters are items that can be included in DOS commands in order to specify additional information for the system. Some parameters are required, others are optional. If you do not include some parameters, a default value will be provided by the system. Examples of some of the parameters you will be working with frequently when using DOS are shown in Figure 3-1.

Parameter	Explanation
[filespec]	A filespec will appear as [d:][filename][.ext]
	Example: B:myfile.doc
	A:yourfile
	anyfiles.bas
	thisfile
	An explanation of each part of the filespec follows.
[d:]	This parameter is the drive indicator. You enter the drive letter followed by a colon to indicate the intended drive. If the drive designation is omitted, DOS will assume that the intended drive is the default drive.
[filename]	You may assign any name to a file as long as it meets the following criteria. The name assigned to the file can have from 1 to 8 characters. The only valid characters are: A-Z 0-9 $ & @ % __ - ( ) ' ' { } # ! (spaces are not allowed)
	The filename parameters are in force even when using application software. The application software may restrict usage to alphabetic and numeric characters and only a few of the other symbols. Check the application software documentation for such rules. If you do use an invalid character, you will receive an error message and then be prompted in some way to use a different filename.
[.ext]	You may assign an optional filename extension with from 1 to 3 characters. If you specify an extension, it must be separated from the filename by a period. Sometimes you cannot specify an extension since some application programs do so automatically.
	Again, the valid characters shown for filenames are also the only valid characters that can be used for extensions. If an extension is assigned, you must include it as part of the filespec whenever you want the system to locate the file.

Figure 3-1 DOS Parameters for Filenames

BACKGROUND ON DIRECTORY COMMAND

The directory command tells the system to display a listing of all the names of the files stored on the disk in the specified drive. It is possible to display a directory of a disk in any drive on the system. You might think of the directory as a table of contents for the disk. It can tell you the names of the files that are on the disk, how much space (bytes) each file is using on the disk, and the date and time the file was created or last modified (that is, if you provided the system with the correct date and time when you started; otherwise, it will give the last date set on the system).

The directory will also indicate the volume identification (if there is one) (you'll learn about volume labels a little later in your training) and the amount of free space left on the disk.

GUIDED ACTIVITY: DISPLAY A DIRECTORY OF ALL FILES ON DISK IN DEFAULT DRIVE

1. Follow the start-up procedures to once again load DOS.

2. Place the **Understanding and Using MS-DOS/PC DOS** training disk in the appropriate data drive for your system (drive A for hard disks and *drive B for floppy drive systems*).

   Be sure to enter the date and time if necessary. When the system prompt (C> or A>) is on the screen, and the cursor is blinking next to it, you will be ready to continue.

   You will first display a directory of the disk that is in the default drive (drive C on hard disk systems and *drive A on floppy drive systems*). The directory will provide a list of the names of the files that are stored on the DOS disk.

3. Type **DIR C:**

   [*If you are using a floppy drive system type* **DIR A:**]

   Note: It is not necessary to type the drive designation when you want to use the default drive such as drive C (*or drive A*) in this example. However, using the drive designation at this point in your training usually makes the drive designation concept a little clearer.

4. Press **<CR>**

   Notice that the in-use light on the drive you indicated in the command comes on briefly as the system looks at that disk to find out what files it contains. (Some hard disks do not display an in-use light.) A list of the files appears on the screen and will look similar to the list shown in Figure 3-2. (Different versions of DOS may have a few differences in the files stored on disk.)

5. End of this guided activity. Continue on to the next section.

```
Volume in drive A is DOS
Directory of  A:\

          COMMAND  COM    23948    3-07-88    3:18p
          CONFIG   SYS       22    1-01-80   12:00a
          AUTOEXEC BAT       16    1-03-89   11:10a
          ASSIGN   COM     1523   12-22-87   10:40a
          CHKDSK   COM     9819    5-02-88    2:53p
          DEBUG    COM    15786    5-02-88    2:53p
          SELECT   COM    10781    9-11-87   10:24a
          EXE2BIN  EXE     2684    5-02-88    2:53p
          FIND     EXE     1986    5-02-88    2:53p
          PRINT    COM     9379   12-22-87    9:35a
          RECOVER  COM     4284    5-02-88    2:53p
          SHARE    EXE     5808    5-02-88    2:53p
          SYS      COM     4687   12-22-87    9:37a
          FORMAT   COM    11562    3-23-88   10:37a
          SORT     EXE     1474    5-02-88    2:54p
          GRAFTABL COM     8689    5-02-88    2:54p
          LABEL    COM     2897    5-02-88    2:54p
          JOIN     EXE     9606   12-22-87   11:01a
          SUBST    EXE    10492   12-22-87   11:08a
          MORE     COM      282   12-22-87   11:02a
          REPLACE  EXE     4852   12-22-87   11:05a
          APPEND   COM     1725   12-22-87   10:39a
          XCOPY    EXE     5402   12-22-87   11:09a
          DISKCOMP COM     6233    5-02-88    8:46a
          DISKCOPY COM     6759    5-02-88    8:46a
          CONFIGUR COM    24832    9-10-87    8:51p
          DSKSETUP COM    23262    3-01-88    4:38p
          MODE     COM    14746    4-14-88    8:54a
          SEARCH   COM     4343   12-22-87   10:34a
          APPLY    COM     2207   10-16-87   10:18a
          TREE     COM     2083   12-22-87   10:34a
          COMP     COM     3759   10-16-87   10:28a
          ANSI     SYS     1651   12-22-87   11:10a
          DRIVER   SYS     1102   12-22-87   11:10a
          BOOTF    COM      188   10-16-87   10:25a
          ZSPOOL   COM     3004   12-22-87   10:35a
          NOSTACK  COM      170    9-12-87    3:28p
          VDISK    SYS     3110    4-06-88   11:27a
          ZCACHE   SYS     4934   11-11-87    2:44p
          39 File(s)  37888 bytes free
```

Figure 3-2, Sample Directory of DOS 3.2 Files

GUIDED ACTIVITY: DISPLAY A DIRECTORY OF THE FILES STORED ON THE UNDERSTANDING AND USING MS-DOS/PC DOS TRAINING DISK IN DATA DRIVE

You now need to see what files are stored on the **Understanding and Using MS-DOS/PC DOS** training disk. Since that disk is not in the default drive, you will have to be absolutely sure to include a drive designation when you type the command.

1. Type **DIR A:**

    [*If you are using a floppy drive system type DIR B:*]

2.   Press **<CR>**

A listing of the names of the files located on the disk in the specified data drive will appear on the screen. Do you see CALENDAR.BAS on the screen or did the filenames move too fast? Well if it's not there and you didn't see it, don't worry. We don't think you'll have to enroll in a speed reading course just yet. The next version of the directory command may help.

3.   End of this guided activity. Continue on to the next section.

BACKGROUND ON PAUSING A DIRECTORY

You can add a parameter to the directory command that will cause the directory to pause before any of the filenames scroll off the top of the screen. Only 24 lines can fit on most microcomputer displays. As additional lines are added to the screen, the lines move off the top of the screen and then disappear. This motion is known as **scrolling**.

You can stop the screen from scrolling at any time when you are using DOS by pressing and holding **Ctrl + NumLock** or **Ctrl + S**. However, when you are displaying a directory, you can use a **/P** parameter with the command and the display will pause so that you can read all of the lines in the directory before any scroll off of the screen.

GUIDED ACTIVITY: DISPLAY AND PAUSE A DIRECTORY OF DISK IN DATA DRIVE

Remember, you still want to see if the CALENDAR.BAS file is on the disk in the data drive.

1.   Type **DIR A: /P**

*[If you are using a floppy drive system type **DIR B: /P**]*

2.   Press **<CR>**

The first group of lines that will fit on the screen will be displayed. (Figure 3-3)

3.   Look for **CALENDAR.BAS**

When you are looking at the listed filenames, remember that the first column of the directory lists the filename for each file stored on the disk in the designated drive. The second column indicates the extension (if any was assigned) for that filename. The third column tells how many bytes the file is using on the disk. The fourth and fifth columns indicate the date and the time when the file was created or last updated. The system uses the date and time that was timestamped onto the file. You will notice that DOS changes the 24-hour format to a.m. and p.m. time.

There is a message at the bottom of the screen telling you what to do when you want to have the listing continue to scroll on the screen. After you have located the filename you are looking for (CALENDAR.BAS), follow the instructions from the screen message.

4.   Strike the appropriate key to continue. (You may have to strike a key one more time to get to the end of the listing.)

5. End of this guided activity. Continue on to the next section.

```
        1AR         WKS      229      1-03-89    9:56a
        CALENDAR    BAS     7040     12-23-85    7:49a
        2AR         WKS      229      1-03-89    9:56a
        BANK        BAS      512     12-01-85    5:29p
        MENU        BAS     1152      1-01-80    5:08a
        AUTOEXEC    BAT       26     12-01-85    5:13p
        3AR         WKS      229      1-03-89    9:56a
        AVERAGES    BAS     1024     12-01-85    5:01p
        TIME        BAS     1792     12-01-85    5:23p
        WONDERS     BAS      896     12-01-85    1:07p
        AUTOEXEC    BAS        1     12-01-85    5:12p
        2SIDEDSK              62     11-27-85   10:33a
        ORDER       BAS      640     12-01-85    4:27p
        SQUARE      BAS      640     12-01-85    4:25p
        FIBONACI    BAS      768     12-01-85    4:27p
        BOOT                 116     12-30-85    7:47a
        MELLOW      BAS     2816     12-01-85    4:34p
        CONFIG               166     12-30-85    7:48a
        DEFAULT              260     11-27-85    8:23a
        CPU                  116     12-30-85    7:49a
        COLDBOOT              60     12-30-85    7:53a
        EXTERNAL             193     11-27-85   10:24a
        BYTE                  80     12-30-85    7:54a
        Strike a key when ready . . .
```

Figure 3-3, Paused Directory of **Understanding and Using MS-DOS/PC DOS** Training Disk (The filenames may appear in a different order on your screen.)

BACKGROUND ON WIDE DISPLAY DIRECTORIES

There may be times when you are simply trying to determine the contents of a disk and you are only interested in the names of the files. This task is easier if all the names are displayed on the screen at the same time. It is possible to use the /W parameter with the directory command in order to produce a wide display that will list the names of the files horizontally across the screen along with any extension that may have been assigned to the filename. The wide display will not indicate the amount of space a file is using on the disk, nor will it include the date and time information.

GUIDED ACTIVITY: DISPLAY A WIDE DIRECTORY OF THE DISK IN THE DATA DRIVE

1. Type **DIR A: /W**

    [If you are using a floppy drive system type DIR B: /W]

2. Press **<CR>**

    A wide display similar to Figure 3-4 will appear on the screen. You will notice that all the filenames are listed along with any assigned extensions. There is no indication of how much space each file uses or the date and time when the file was created or last updated. (Do you see CALENDAR.BAS?)

3. End of this guided activity. Continue on to the next section.

```
Volume in drive A has no label
Directory of  A:\

1AR          WKS   CALENDAR   BAS   2AR         WKS   BANK        BAS   MENU        BAS
AUTOEXEC BAT       3AR        WKS   AVERAGES    BAS   TIME        BAS   WONDERS     BAS
AUTOEXEC BAS       2SIDEDSK         ORDER       BAS   SQUARE      BAS   FIBONACI    BAS
BOOT               MELLOW     BAS   CONFIG            DEFAULT           CPU
COLDBOOT           EXTERNAL         BYTE              FILENAME          RESET
DIR                FILE       EXT                     BACKUP            COPY
COMPUTER BAS       PROG       FIL   DATABASE FIL      DOCUMENT FIL      COPY        1
COPY        2      COPY       3     AR1         WKS   AR2         WKS   AR3         WKS
FILE1       PIC    FILE2      PIC   FILE3       PIC   AR1         PIC   AR2         PIC
AR3         PIC    1AR        WK1   2AR         WK1   3AR         WK1   AR1         WK1
AR2         WK1    AR3        WK1   NEWABC      DBF   NEWABC      DBT   ABC1        DBF
ABC1        DBT    BLAIRLIN   DOC   LIB         DOC   LEASE       KEY   MEMO1
MEMO2              MEMO3
     62 File(s)     260096 bytes free
```

Figure 3-4, Wide Directory of **Understanding and Using MS-DOS/PC DOS** Training Disk
(The filenames may appear in a different order on your screen.)

BACKGROUND ON A DIRECTORY LISTING A SPECIFIED FILENAME

You have been looking for the filename "CALENDAR.BAS" in the last few directories that you've done. The longer the directory listing is, the more difficult it may be to find the name of a file you need. It is possible to add a filename when entering the DIR command so that only the specified filename information will appear in the listing. If the file is not stored where you asked DOS to look for it (ex. if it's not on the disk in drive A), DOS will display a "File not found" message.

GUIDED ACTIVITY: DO A DIRECTORY LISTING CALENDAR.BAS

You want to see if CALENDAR.BAS is stored on the disk in the data drive.

1. Type **DIR A:CALENDAR.BAS**

    *[If you are using a floppy drive system type **DIR B:CALENDAR.BAS**]*

2. Press **<CR>**

If you typed the command correctly (check spelling and spacing), and you spelled the name of the file correctly and included the period followed by the extension, a listing similar to the following should appear on the screen:

```
Volume in drive A is LASTNAME
Directory of A:\

CALENDAR     BAS        7040        12-23-85      7:49a
    1 File(s)  260096
```

3.   End of this guided activity. Continue on to the next section.

BACKGROUND ON A SORTED DIRECTORY

As you will notice, the names listed in the directories do not seem to be arranged in any special order. As a directory grows, it becomes more difficult to sort through the different filenames in an effort to determine exactly which files are stored on the disk. You can use the directory command along with the SORT command to arrange the names of the files alphabetically on the screen. The alphabetic order is based only on the first letter of each filename. The SORT command will not rearrange the files on the disk, only the filenames on the screen will be in alphabetical order. (See Figure 3-5)

It is also possible to sort the filenames according to the extensions, or according to the size of the file, or the date, or the time by adding a column number to the command. You will not display that type of sorted directory as part of your guided activities. If you are interested in finding out more about how this can be accomplished, check the DOS documentation under the "SORT" command information.

NOTE: The following guided activity should be done ONLY if you are using a hard disk system. If you are using a floppy disk system, you are most likely using a write-protected DOS disk (the write-protect notch is covered on 5-1/4" disks or uncovered on the 3-1/2" disk). In order to use the SORT command, DOS must be able to write data to the disk (temporarily) and it cannot do so if the disk is write protected. You can read the following steps and then look at Figure 3-5 to see the results of the command, but, do not do this command unless you are using a hard disk system or an unprotected DOS program disk on a floppy disk system.

GUIDED ACTIVITY: DISPLAY A SORTED DIRECTORY USING A HARD DISK SYSTEM

The **Understanding and Using MS-DOS/PC DOS** training disk should be in the data drive (drive A on most hard disk systems)...do not do this activity on a floppy disk system.

1.   Type **DIR A: ¦ SORT**

     The split bar (sometimes referred to as the "piping" symbol) is the shift of the backslash key on most keyboards.

2.   Press **<CR>**

     The system will take a few seconds to alphabetize the filenames and then list the names on the screen. Notice that the names do appear in alphabetic order (Figure 3-5).

3.   End of this guided activity. Continue on to the next section.

BACKGROUND ON CLEAR SCREEN COMMAND

By this time your screen is pretty full. You probably have information displayed from the last activity or two. Whenever you want to clear the screen for new information, simply type CLS and press the Return key.

```
DIR A: ¦ SORT
Directory of  A:\
Volume in drive A has no label
1AR        WK1      235      1-03-89    10:02a
1AR        WKS      229      1-03-89     9:56a
2AR        WK1      235      1-03-89    10:02a
2AR        WKS      229      1-03-89     9:56a
2SIDEDSK            62      11-27-85    10:33a
3AR        WK1      235      1-03-89    10:02a
3AR        WKS      229      1-03-89     9:56a
ABC1       DBF       76      1-03-89    10:07a
ABC1       DBT      126      1-03-89    10:08a
AR1        PIC      226      1-03-89     9:59a
AR1        WK1      235      1-03-89    10:02a
AR1        WKS      229      1-03-89     9:56a
AR2        PIC      226      1-03-89     9:59a
AR2        WK1      235      1-03-89    10:02a
AR2        WKS      229      1-03-89     9:56a
AR3        PIC      226      1-03-89     9:59a
AR3        WK1      235      1-03-89    10:02a
AR3        WKS      229      1-03-89     9:56a
AUTOEXEC   BAS        1     12-01-85     5:12p
AUTOEXEC   BAT       26     12-01-85     5:13p
AVERAGES   BAS     1024     12-01-85     5:01p
BACKUP             328     12-30-85     8:01a
BANK       BAS      512     12-01-85     5:29p
BLAIRLIN   DOC      561      1-03-89    10:09a
BOOT               116     12-30-85     7:47a
BYTE                80     12-30-85     7:54a
CALENDAR   BAS     7040     12-23-85     7:49a
COLDBOOT            60     12-30-85     7:53a
COMPUTER   BAS     7040     12-23-85     7:49a
CONFIG             166     12-30-85     7:48a
COPY                73     12-30-85     8:01a
COPY         1     155     12-30-85     8:03a
COPY         2     185     12-30-85     8:04a
COPY         3     212     12-30-85     8:05a
```

Figure 3-5, Partial Sorted Directory of **Understanding and Using MS-DOS/PC DOS** Training Disk

GUIDED ACTIVITY: CLEAR THE SCREEN AND DISPLAY A WIDE DIRECTORY

1. Type **CLS**

2. Press **<CR>**

The screen will be erased and the cursor will be positioned next to the DOS prompt in the upper left corner of the screen awaiting your next command. Display the wide directory of the disk in the data drive.

3. Type **DIR A: /W**

   [*If you are using a floppy drive system type* **DIR B: /W**]

4. Press **<CR>**

The wide display of the directory for the disk in the data drive will appear.

5. End of this guided activity. Continue on to the next section.

BACKGROUND ON PRINT SCREEN FUNCTION

A wide directory can be printed and then stored along with the disk so that the disk's contents can easily be determined. Printing a copy of a directory can be done in a few different ways. The method you are going to try out now, however, will print an exact copy of everything that is on the screen.

When performing the print screen function using some keyboards (usually the 84-key keyboard style), you will have to use the <SHIFT> + PrtSc keystrokes. If you are using another type of keyboard such as the 101 keys keyboard style, you may find a Print Screen key that will perform the print screen function with the single keystroke. If you are not sure which will work on your system, try the single keystroke (Print Screen). If it doesn't work, use the <SHIFT> + PrtSc combination. Whatever is on the screen when you use the print screen function will be printed on paper.

You may find it helpful to use this function if you are using tutorial disks that provide information on the screen that you would like to study, or to print information from a help screen that may be available within the application software you use. Rather than taking notes, just print a copy of the screen. Or, if you are working on a project and you want to ask someone a question about something that is on the screen, you can print a copy and take it with you so that you can get an answer to your question.

BACKGROUND ON CHECKING TO BE SURE PRINTER IS ONLINE

In order for any printing function to work, check to be sure that your printer is turned on and online. With the wide variety of printers that is available, our best recommendation is that you become familiar with the printer you are using through the printer user's manual. Familiarize yourself with how the printer indicates if its power is on or off and how it indicates whether or not the printer is online. It is very possible that a printer can be turned on and not be online.

If the printer is not online, it cannot receive messages from the microcomputer system to do your printing. Some software programs are quite forgiving if you forget to put the printer online before you send something to be printed. Other programs, however, are not quite as nice. They may make you give all the printing instructions over again once the printer is online, or worse yet, simply stop working so that you have to reload the program and possibly lose some data in the process.

Usually a printer will have lights to indicate when the power is on and when it is online and have buttons to press to achieve the on or off status.

If you are using a microcomputer that shares a printer with other microcomputers, you will have additional checking to do. Not only must you check to be sure that the printer is turned on and online, you must be sure that your microcomputer is the one that is switched to print. Since this sharing procedure varies greatly, be sure to check with your instructor for the appropriate guidelines.

GUIDED ACTIVITY: PRINT THE SCREEN

You should have the wide display of the directory for the **Understanding and Using MS-DOS/PC DOS** training disk on the screen. You will now print a copy of the screen using the Print Screen function.

1. Press the **Print Screen** key.

   If that does not work do the following:

   While you hold down the **<SHIFT>**, tap the **PrtSc** key.

2. Release the Key(s).

   An exact copy of the screen will print.

3. End of this guided activity. Continue on to the next section.

GUIDED ACTIVITY: REMOVE PAPER FROM PRINTER

Your instructor may want you to turn in a copy of the printed screen. If you need the printed copy, you are going to have to remove the paper from the printer. Again, it will be important for you to become familiar with the printer you are using. You must locate the form feed button(s). Some printers call these buttons "form feed" or "FF" or "top of page" (you can see why you will have to look at the printer you are using and/or check the printer manual to be sure you are using the correct paper advancement procedures). The procedure to follow for many dot matrix printers is:

1. Press the **form feed** button to advance the paper.

   If this technique works, the paper will advance the length of one sheet of paper. Some printers have to be off-line in order for the form feed to work. If you are using that type of printer, do this:

   Press the **online** button on the printer to take the printer offline. Most printers have toggle-type buttons to accomplish this. Then, press the **form feed** button to advance the paper. **Do not turn the roller knobs to advance the paper when the printer's power is turned on...this can strip the gears. If you must use the roller knobs, be sure to turn off the power to the printer.**

2. You may want to press **form feed** a second time to advance the paper far enough so that you can tear it off easily.

3. Tear the paper off at the perforation if you are using a continuous-feed type of printer.

   Many organizations would prefer that you not use the plastic shield on the printer to tear off the paper because the pulverized paper residue will fall into the printer. It may be better to advance the paper far enough to tear off at the perforation even if it means advancing an extra blank sheet of paper.

4. If you had to take the printer off-line to form feed the paper, press the **online** button to put the printer back online.

5. Label the printout with your name and "Unit 3, Print Screen".

6. End of this guided activity. Continue on to the next section.

BACKGROUND ON OUTPUT TO PRINTER FUNCTION

There may be times when you want everything that you type on the keyboard to appear on the screen and also to print on paper. For example, if you want a complete directory of the **Understanding and Using MS-DOS/PC DOS** training disk including the disk space used and the date and time information, the print screen function could not provide it. Several of the lines of the directory scroll off the screen and so could not be captured on paper using the print screen function. The output to the printer function will allow you to direct your keystrokes not only to the screen but also to the printer.

There will be times later in this book when you will be instructed to send your output to the printer so that your instructor will have a record of what you have done. You can accomplish that output by using the output to printer function.

GUIDED ACTIVITY: OUTPUT TO PRINTER

When you activate this function, nothing will appear to happen. However, as soon as you begin to use the keyboard, you should get a response from the printer. If you press the keys that will activate the output to printer function and then press those same keys a second time, you will immediately deactivate the function (remember, those are called "toggle" keystrokes... press once to turn the function on, press again to turn the function off).

1. Check to be sure the printer is online (and if you are sharing a printer check to be sure that it is switched to your microcomputer).

2. Press and hold the **Ctrl** key.

3. Tap the **PrtSc** key.

4. Release both keys immediately.

   (Please note that tapping the letter "p" rather than the PrtSc key will have the same effect.)

5. In order to see if the function has be activated, press **<CR>** a few times.

   You should hear the printer click as you press the Return key and a few other things might happen depending upon the version of DOS you are using. You will see a system prompt appear on the screen (and possibly print on paper) for each time you pressed the Return key. You are not concerned with those prompts and they will not interfere with what you are doing. You are simply using the returns to check that the output is going to the printer. With some printers, such as laser printers, the only evidence that you will have that output is going to the printer is that the "form feed" light (or some other light) will turn on to indicate that there is something in the printer's buffer.

6. If you do not get any printer response, repeat steps 1 through 5.

    When the output to printer function has been activated, you will be ready to continue.

7. Type **DIR A:**

    [*If you are using a floppy drive system type* **DIR B:**]

8. Press **<CR>**

9. When the printer stops printing, use the proper paper removal techniques to remove the printed directory. If necessary, put the printer back online.

10. Label the printout with your name and "Unit 3, Output to Printer".

11. End of this guided activity. Continue on to the next section.

GUIDED ACTIVITY: DEACTIVATE OUTPUT TO PRINTER

You now want to stop the output to printer. Until you deactivate the output to printer function, everything that you type on the keyboard will appear on the display and print on paper. (If you are sharing the printer, the others sharing it with you may become annoyed if you tie up printer usage for too long a period.)

1. Hold down the **Ctrl** key.

2. Tap the **PrtSc** key.

3. Release both keys.

    (Remember, tapping the letter "p" rather than the PrtSc key will have the same effect.) If you are using a laser printer, you may have to form feed the paper to clear the printer.

4. Press **<CR>** a few times.

    There should be no response from the printer when you press the Return key if you deactivated the output to printer function. If there is a response, repeat steps 1 through 4.

5. If you are going to stop working now, follow the appropriate shut-down procedures (pg. 32-33).

6. Last guided activity in this unit.

REVIEW QUESTIONS

1. Is it acceptable to put a space in a filename?

    No - a error message will appear.
    (8 characters to a file name)
    No spaces of extended its joined by a period.

too many

2. Which of the following are acceptable filenames?

   REPORT1 ✓   JOHNSONMEMO   BENSON.LTR ✓
   1.2 ✓   MYFILE.1 ✓   LETTER|8.DOC

3. You want to do a directory of the disk in drive B. Write the command exactly as you would type it.   _DIR B:_

4. What is a file?   _a file is all information with which a computer works._

5. How are the results of this command -- DIR B: /P -- different from the results of this command -- DIR B: /W -- ?   _DIR B: /P - this one pauses directory_
   DIR B: /W - is wide directory

6. How are the results of these two commands different? DIR A: DIR A: ¦ SORT

7. What keystrokes do you use if you want to print an exact copy of the screen?
   print screen   or   ctrl (hold) + prt Sc.

8. What keystrokes do you use in order to activate the output to printer function?
   CTL + hold print screen } → toggle ① on ② off   process   DIR B:↵

9. What happens immediately after you activate the output to printer function?
   printer prints

10. If you activate the output to printer function and then type **DIR A:** and press the Return key and the directory is only listed on the screen rather than also printing on paper, what might be wrong? _- you may have held the button too long, - maybe typed incorrectly, - is printer on?_

DOCUMENTATION RESEARCH

1. What is a device error message?

2. If the error message says "Abort, Retry, Ignore?", what would a response with each of the options do?

   a. Abort

   b. Retry

   c. Ignore

3. If a disk or device error occurs at any time during a command or a program, DOS will display an error message. Look in the DOS documentation to find out information about these messages.

   a. Why would you receive a "Data error" message?

   b. Why would you receive a "General failure error" message?

   c. Why would you receive a "No paper error" message?

   d. Why would you receive a "Not ready error" message?

   e. Why would you receive a "Read fault error", "Sector not found error", or "Seek error" message?

   f. Why would you receive a "Write protect error" message?

4. What command can you use to sort a directory based on the date?

5. What command can you use to sort a directory based on the file size?

UNIT
4 A LOOK AT MENUS AND FILES

SUPPLIES NEEDED

In order to complete this unit, you will need:

1. this book;
2. the **Understanding and Using MS-DOS/PC DOS** training disk.

OBJECTIVES

After completing this unit you will be able to:

1. define **main menu**;
2. define **submenu**;
3. make a selection from a menu;
4. make a selection from a submenu;
5. follow screen prompts;
6. send a file to the printer;
7. adjust paper in the printer;
8. define exit procedures;
9. follow proper exit procedures;
10. stop output to printer.

ASSIGNMENTS

1. _____ Printed Calendar
2. _____ Review Questions
3. _____ Documentation Research

BACKGROUND ON A MENU

A **menu** is a list of activities that many software programs provide to help the user move from one activity to another. Many programs display a menu immediately after they are loaded. Some programs allow you to access menus once you are in the program through function keys or other specified keystrokes.

The first menu that is displayed after loading a software program is usually referred to as the **main menu**. Other menus that may branch off from the **main menu** are referred to as **submenus**.

GUIDED ACTIVITY: LOAD THE UNDERSTANDING AND USING MS-DOS/PC DOS TRAINING DISK

1. Insert the **Understanding and Using MS-DOS/PC DOS** training disk in drive A. You will not need a data disk for this activity.

2. Make sure that the printer connected to your microcomputer is online for your workstation.

3. If the microcomputer is turned off, perform a cold boot to load the program (remember, just turn on the power switch). If the microcomputer is on, perform a warm boot to load the program (press and hold the **Ctrl + Alt** keys. Then press the **Del** key. Release all three keys).

   The program will begin to load.

4. Enter the date and time when prompted to do so.

   After you enter the date and time correctly, the program will continue to load and a menu will appear on the screen. See Figure 4-1.

5. End of this guided activity. Continue on to the next section.

BACKGROUND ON MAKING A MENU SELECTION

Figure 4-1 illustrates the main menu that will appear when you load the **Understanding and Using MS-DOS/PC DOS** training disk. Several popular application software programs will use a main menu to help guide the user through the various functions offered by the program. The disk that accompanies the **Understanding and Using MS-DOS/PC DOS** book was created largely to provide you with data files to manipulate with DOS commands. It was not created to provide an example of good programming techniques but can be used as an introduction to using menus and following screen prompts.

Notice that there are ten choices on the main menu numbered from one through ten. The directions for making your selection read as follows: "Enter Number of Your Choice, Then Press Return." Notice that one of the selections is "Calendar." Does the name "Calendar" sound familiar? It should, because that is the name of the file that we have pointed out to you several times.

You are going to select "5" from the main menu in order to select the "Calendar" option. You will first print a "computer" and then, without advancing the paper, you will print a calendar so that when you are finished you will have printed a computer calendar.

UNDERSTANDING AND USING MS-DOS/PC DOS

```
1.    SQUARE ROOT OF A NUMBER
2.    ORDER THREE NUMBERS
3.    COMPUTER CONFIGURATION
4.    FIBONACCI SEQUENCE
5.    CALENDAR
6.    SAVING PENNIES
7.    THE TIME
8.    FIGURING BOWLING AVERAGES
9.    HAVE YOU NEVER BEEN MELLOW?
10.   END OF WORK SESSION

ENTER NUMBER OF CHOICE, THEN PRESS RETURN? ___
```

Figure 4-1, Main Menu for the **Understanding and Using MS-DOS/PC DOS** Training Disk

This exercise will serve several purposes. It will allow you to make selections from a main menu and from a submenu, to follow screen prompts, to send a file to the printer, and then to follow the proper exit procedures from a program. It will also give you practice in following written instructions (a skill needed to complete projects with written guidelines or to follow the directions given in a software program's documentation), a crucial skill for any microcomputer user. In the process, you might even have a little fun.

GUIDED ACTIVITY: MAKE SELECTION FROM MAIN MENU

1. Make sure that you are at the main menu shown in Figure 4-1.

2. Type **5**

3. Press **<CR>**   A submenu will appear. See Figure 4-2.

4. End of this guided activity. Continue on to the next section.

BACKGROUND ON ADJUSTING PAPER IN PRINTER

In order to get your printout to print on the page without crossing the perforation, it may be necessary to adjust the paper in your printer when using a continuous feed printer. To do this, it is first necessary to turn off the printer attached to your workstation. Then, you may check with the printer manual or lab assistant to find out how to align the top of the paper correctly. On many printers, turning the roller knob on the printer until the perforation at the top of the paper is aligned with the top of the printer ribbon will line the paper up correctly. It is important to note that the roller knobs on a printer should not be turned unless the printer's power is turned off (it is not enough for the printer to be offline).

```
Enter the number of your selection and then press Return:

1)  Computer
2)  Calendar
3)  Return to Main Menu

If you wish to print a computer first, and then print a calendar,
first choose Computer, and then without advancing the paper in the printer,
choose calendar.

TYPE 1, 2, OR 3?  ___
```

Figure 4-2, Submenu to Print Calendar

GUIDED ACTIVITY: PRINT COMPUTER FOR COMPUTER CALENDAR

Make sure that you are at the submenu (see Figure 4-2). The prompt at the top of the screen indicates that you should "Enter the number of your selection and then press Return."

1. Type **1**   This will select "Computer."

2. Press **<CR>**

A facsimile of a computer will print. Do not remove the paper from the printer at this point.

3. Type **2**   This will select "Calendar."

4. Press **<CR>**

You will be asked to "Enter Year?". When you enter the year, enter the full year. For example, enter "1991" rather than "91." Remember to use the top row of numbers on the keyboard (you cannot substitute the lowercase "L" for the "1").

5. Enter the year that you want your calendar to represent.

6. Press **<CR>**

The following prompt will appear: "Please wait...I'm calculating your custom calendar." In a moment, the calendar will start to print.

7. When the calendar stops printing, use the correct procedures to remove the paper from the printer.

8. End of this guided activity. Continue on to the next section.

BACKGROUND ON EXIT PROCEDURES

When you finish a work session, some software programs require that you follow some sort of exit procedure. The exit procedure often specifies that you should save the file on which you are working to the disk and return to a special screen or to the main menu. Other programs may instruct you to return to the DOS prompt before you remove your disks in order to close any files that might be open. It is important for you to be aware of and to follow exit procedures as required by the software you are using in order to minimize the possibility of losing data.

BACKGROUND ON A BASIC PROGRAM

The little program that you just used was prepared using a programming language called Basica. When follow the menu directions to exit the program, you will be in an area where you could write some of these Basic programs. So, when you exit you will be in Basic. While there, you will "play" a little with the CALENDAR.BAS file. You will "load" the file into the system's memory and then "list" the lines that make up the program. When you are in Basic, you can only load and list files that were written using the Basic programming language.

GUIDED ACTIVITY: EXITING FROM UNDERSTANDING AND USING MS-DOS/PC DOS TRAINING DISK PROGRAM

The cursor should be located at the **Understanding and Using MS-DOS/PC DOS** training disk calendar submenu (see Figure 4-2).

1. Type **3**   This will select "Return to Main Menu"

2. Press **<CR>**   The program will return to the Main Menu.

3. Type **10**   This will select "END WORK SESSION"

4. Press **<CR>**

A few notes of music will play and the following message will appear on the screen. "Good-Bye. Hope to work with you again". An "ok" will appear on the screen. This is Basic's prompt. At this point you could remove (but please don't remove it yet) the **Understanding and Using MS-DOS/PC DOS** training disk from the drive and follow your shut-down procedures. For the moment, leave the disk in the drive.

5. End of this guided activity. Continue on to the next section.

BACKGROUND ON THE FUNCTION KEYS IN BASIC

Remember the ten or twelve function keys located on the left side of the keyboard (or across the top of the keyboard)? In our discussion of the keyboard, we told you that we couldn't define for you what each specific key does because each program can assign a different function for each key. Now you will finally get a chance to use some of these keys. When you exited the **Understanding and Using MS-DOS/PC DOS** training disk program, the program put you in Basic. In Basic, function key F3 will allow you to load a file that contains a Basic program. The F1 key will allow you to list the contents of that Basic program. You will use those keys in the next guided activity. Remember, though, these functions are only assigned to those keys when you are using Basica. Other programs will assign different tasks to these function keys.

BACKGROUND ON LOOKING AT A FILE

You are going to look at the CALENDAR.BAS file that you just used to print the calendar. You might think of the next guided activity as the electronic equivalent of opening a file folder to look through its contents.

GUIDED ACTIVITY: LOOK AT CALENDAR.BAS FILE

The main menu should be on the screen with the exit message displayed. The last thing displayed on the screen should be "ok" with the cursor at the bottom of the screen.

1. Press the **F3** key.   The word "LOAD" will appear.

2. Type **CALENDAR.BAS**

    This is the name of the file that you wish to load.

3. Press **<CR>**

    The word "ok" will appear. Don't worry if you made a mistake when typing the filename, simply repeat steps 1 through 3.

4. Press the **F1** key.   The word "LIST" will appear.

5. Press **<CR>**

    The contents of the CALENDAR.BAS file will scroll onto the screen. By now you have seen the filename CALENDAR.BAS displayed on the screen when you did a directory, you have actually used the program in order to print a calendar, and here you have looked at the actual contents of the file. This CALENDAR.BAS file might look a little more like a file to you if you printed it, put the printed copy into a file folder labeled *CALENDAR.BAS*, and filed it in a file cabinet. Some individuals like to think of the disk as being a little electronic file cabinet in which various files can be stored.

    You now want to return to DOS and its system prompt.   The Basic "ok" is on the screen and the cursor is below it.

6. Type **SYSTEM**

7. Press **<CR>**

    The DOS prompt appears on the screen.

8. Remove the **Understanding and Using MS-DOS/PC DOS** training disk from drive A and put it into its protective envelope.

9. Last guided activity in this unit.

REVIEW QUESTIONS

1. What does a main menu allow you to do?

   move from one activity to another through a list of activities

2. When will you see a program's submenu?

   Usually when the program is first loaded or when the function keys are used.

3. Why is it important to follow a program's exit procedures?

4. Will the function keys perform the same functions in every program you use? Why or why not?

5. Explain why a disk is sometimes compared to a file cabinet.

6. How do you know if the paper in the printer you are using is aligned correctly? (Answers will vary according to type of printer so specify which type of printer you are explaining. If more than one, specify each one.)

DOCUMENTATION RESEARCH

1. What does it mean to format a disk with the system on it? Write out the exact command.

2. What does it mean to format a disk with a volume label. Write out the exact command.

3. Can you use the diskcopy command on a hard disk? If so, how will it differ from a floppy-drive system?

4. What are the advantages of using a file-by-file copy instead of the diskcopy command?

5. What are the advantages of using the XCOPY command?

6. List three internal commands.

7. List three external commands.

8. What will the following command accomplish?

    COPY A:YOURPROG.123 B:MYPROG.456

NOTES:

UNIT
5 COPYING FILES ONTO A FORMATTED DISK

SUPPLIES NEEDED

In order to complete this unit, you will need:

1. this book;
2. DOS command program files;
3. the **Understanding and Using MS-DOS/PC DOS** training disk files;
4. blank data disk.

OBJECTIVES

After completing this unit you will be able to:

1. format a disk;
2. recognize DOS messages if a disk is not formatted;
3. identify the consequences of formatting a disk;
4. copy one file;
5. copy using the global or wildcard character;
6. copy all files from one disk to another using Copy *.* command.

IMPORTANT KEYSTROKES AND COMMANDS

The important keystrokes and commands that will be introduced in this unit are:
Note: **d** = designated drive   **filename** = name of file   **ext** = name of extension

1. Format a disk in designated drive .... FORMAT d: <CR>
2. Copy one file from source drive to target .... COPY d:filename.ext d: <CR>
3. Copy files with same filename
       from source drive to target .... COPY d:filename.* d: <CR>

4. Copy files with same extension
      from source drive to target .... COPY d:*.ext d: <CR>
5. Copy all files from source drive to target .... COPY d:*.* d: <CR>

ASSIGNMENTS

1. _____✓_____   Review Questions
2. _____   Documentation Research

BACKGROUND ON ACCESSING DOS AND TRAINING FILES ON HARD DISK SYSTEMS AND FLOPPY DISK SYSTEMS

You are about to use some more DOS commands. In order to do so, you will have to be sure that DOS is loaded and that the system prompt is on the screen.

Hard Disk System users will have to check with their instructor to find out what procedures to follow in order to access the DOS command programs and the files from the **Understanding and Using MS-DOS/PC DOS** training disk. There are many possible configurations for the installation of DOS and the training disk files on a hard disk. Some hard disk systems will display a menu when they are started. From that menu you might be instructed to select a "DOS Training" option which will put you in a section where the training disk files will be available as well as the DOS command programs that you will need. Other hard disk systems will just present you with the system prompt and you will have to type in a command or two to get to the section that will give you access to the files you need. Please ask your instructor or lab assistant how to proceed on the hard disk you are using. Once you know what the procedure is, you can follow it whenever you are told that you must have the DOS files and/or the **Understanding and Using MS-DOS/PC DOS** files available.

Floppy Disk System users will have to put the DOS program disk in drive A and then boot the system (follow the startup procedures outlined in Unit 2). You will then be instructed which disks to use in each of the guided activities.

You will need your own blank disk regardless of the type of system you use.

GUIDED ACTIVITY: DIRECTORY OF YOUR BLANK DISK

Be sure that you have followed the correct procedures to load DOS and that the DOS command program files are available (see suggestions above). Your blank disk should be in the data drive (drive A on hard disk systems and *drive B on floppy disk systems*).

1. Type **DIR A:**

   [*If you are using a floppy drive system type* **DIR B:**]

2. Press **<CR>**

   An error message similar to the following may appear on the screen. "General Failure error reading drive *d* Abort, Retry, Ignore?" (We will explain this error message in a moment.) If you got a directory listing of the designated disk (**be sure that you did designate the drive where your data disk is located and not the hard disk or the DOS disk**

on a floppy system) or a "File not found" message, you are working with a "used" disk. If you are using a disk that already contains files, you should be aware that the next command will erase all the files on your data disk. This is fine as long as you don't need the files any longer. Also, some of the other messages that we will be describing will be different from those that you might receive if the disk you are using is not "new."

3. If the "Abort, Retry, Ignore" message is still on the screen -- Type A to "abort" the command. End of this guided activity. Continue on to the next section.

 BACKGROUND ON FORMAT COMMAND: Caution -- this command will erase a disk!

If you take a brand new disk and attempt to have the system read from it or write to it, you will receive an error message, just as you may have received in the preceding guided activity. That is because a brand new disk is unusable until you format it for the system you are using. Then the system can read data from and write data to the disk.

The Format command is a DOS command that accomplishes several things. The Format command can be used to prepare a new disk so that it can be used on the system. Format can also be used to erase an entire disk that contains data you no longer need. The disk can then be reused. Unless you wish to use the Format command to erase a disk, you will have to format each disk only once.

If you have any doubt about the contents of the disk you are going to format, display a directory of the disk to make sure that it does not contain any files you want to keep. If you are using a floppy system it is a good idea to write-protect the DOS program disk. You can protect a floppy disk from being accidentally erased or changed by placing a little sticker over the write-protect notch (see Figure 1-6 and Figure 1-7, page 11). Place one half of the sticker over the write-protect notch on one side of the disk and fold the sticker so that it covers the write-protect notch on the other side of the disk.

If you are using a hard disk system, you must be very careful with this command. In fact, many users will take extra precautions that are beyond the scope of this book to guard against accidentally erasing the hard disk when using this command (such as utilizing a little thing called a "batch" file that will make sure that when the Format command is executed the floppy drive is automatically designated in the command).

 BACKGROUND ON INTERNAL AND EXTERNAL COMMANDS

Earlier in this book we stated that when DOS is loaded, <u>some</u> of the DOS programs are loaded into the machine's memory. The commands that are loaded into the system's memory when DOS is loaded are referred to as **internal** commands. These internal commands can be executed anytime the system prompt is displayed; it does not matter if the DOS disk is present in the default drive. The **internal** commands include (but are not limited to) Chdir, Cls, Copy, Del (Erase), Date, Dir, Mkdir, Ren, Rmdir, Type, Time.

Other DOS commands are not loaded into the machine's memory when DOS is loaded, either because they are used less frequently than some of the other DOS commands and/or because they take up a lot of the system's memory. These commands are referred to as **external** commands. To execute an external command, not only must the system prompt be displayed but the DOS command program files must be readily available. On a hard disk system, access to the external commands is accomplished with proper installation instructions. If you are using a hard disk system, you may not notice any difference between an internal and an external command. The system has already been told where it can find the DOS command files so that when you issue one of the external commands, the system knows where to look for the instructions to carry out the command.

If you are using a floppy system, you simply have to be sure that the DOS program disk is in the default drive. The **external** commands include (but are not limited to): Comp, Chkdsk, Diskcomp, Diskcopy, Format, Sort, and Xcopy. See Figure 5-1 for a summary of the internal and external commands.

Know difference

INTERNAL

COMMAND	FUNCTION
CHDIR (CD)	CHANGE SUBDIRECTORIES OR PRINT CURRENT DIRECTORY
CLS	CLEAR SCREEN
COPY	COPY FILE(S)
DATE	ENTER OR CHANGE DATE KNOWN TO SYSTEM
DEL	ERASE FILE(S)
DIR	LIST NAMES OF FILES STORED ON DISK
ERASE	SAME AS DEL
MKDIR (MD)	MAKE A SUBDIRECTORY
REN	RENAME A FILE
RMDIR (RD)	REMOVE A SUBDIRECTORY
TIME	ENTER OR CHANGE TIME KNOWN TO SYSTEM
TYPE	DISPLAY CONTENTS OF THE SPECIFIED FILE

EXTERNAL

COMMAND	FUNCTION
CHKDSK	CHECK DESIGNATED DRIVE OR DIRECTORY FOR CONSISTENCY, DISPLAYS CONTENTS IN BYTES
DIR ¦ SORT	RUN THE DIRECTORY LISTING OF FILES THROUGH A SORT SO THAT DISPLAY IS ORGANIZED ACCORDING TO FIRST LETTER OF FILENAMES
DISKCOPY	FORMAT A DISK FOR USE, ERASE CONTENTS OF TARGET DISK, COPIES A "MIRROR" IMAGE OF THE SOURCE DISK ONTO THE TARGET DISK
FORMAT	PREPARE A DISK FOR USE ON THE SYSTEM, ERASES CONTENTS OF DISK
TREE	LIST THE PATH OF EACH DIRECTORY AND SUBDIRECTORY ON A DESIGNATED DISK
XCOPY	COPY FILES AND SUBDIRECTORIES

Figure 5-1, Internal and External DOS Commands Discussed in this Book

GUIDED ACTIVITY: FORMAT A DISK

Now that you have done a directory of your data disk to verify that you are using a brand new disk or to be sure that there are no files on the disk that you will need later, you are ready to format the disk.

1. Make sure that DOS is loaded, that the system prompt is displayed, that the DOS command files are available on the hard disk *(or that the DOS disk is in drive A on a floppy system)*, and that your disk is in the data drive (drive A on a hard disk *or drive B on a floppy system*).

2. Type **FORMAT A:**   [*If you are using a floppy drive system type FORMAT B:*]

3. Press **<CR>**

A message similar to the following should appear: "Insert new disk in Drive *d*: and press RETURN when ready." The *d* shown in the message here will actually be the designated drive on the screen. We will be using *d* for the messages we illustrate.

4. Make sure that the disk you wish to format is in the designated drive as shown in the message displayed on the screen.

(Are you sure the message on the screen indicates the drive where the blank disk is located. If the message, for example, tells you to insert the new disk in drive A on the floppy system or indicates drive C on a hard disk system, you should stop what you are doing because you may be well on your way to formatting the wrong disk--disastrous. If the wrong drive is indicated in the system's message, just press and hold the **Ctrl** key and then touch the **Break** key [ScrollLock].) This will stop the command from going any further. You can then retype the format command--with great care--making sure that you have included proper spacing, drive designation, and the colon...not the semicolon.) If you get a message that there is an attempted write-protect violation, make sure that you have specified the correct drive and that the data disk in the drive is not write-protected.

5. If all is well, strike the key as instructed by the DOS program message to begin the formatting process.

A message such as "Formatting..." or a "Head: Cylinder:" count may appear on the screen and remain there while the disk is being formatted. Notice that the drive in-use light is on for the designated drive while the system is formatting your data disk. When the formatting is complete, the screen will look similar to the screen shown in Figure 5-2.

```
    d>  FORMAT d:

        Insert new disk in drive d:
        and press RETURN when ready

        Format complete

              362496 bytes total disk space
              362496 bytes available on disk

        Do you want to format another disk (Y/N)?
```

Figure 5-2, Format Completion Screen

As you can see from Figure 5-2, the screen reveals how much total space is available on the disk, how much space is left on the disk, and whether there are any bad sectors on the disk (your screen may vary slightly depending upon the capacity of your data disk and which version of DOS you are using).

If you have any bytes in bad sectors, try formatting the disk again (see directions in the next paragraph to format another). Sometimes a second or third formatting process will eliminate the bad sectors. If not, return your disk to the store where it was purchased. If the disk is used, you can be pretty sure that the bad sectors have been put aside so that they will not affect your data, however, don't risk anything too important by using a disk that has begun to develop bad areas. It could be the beginning of a growing problem with the disk and your time and data are probably worth more than the cost of a new disk.

When the formatting process is complete, your data disk is ready to be used with the system. You will be asked if you wish to format another disk. If you wish to format another disk (or the same disk a second time in order to get rid of bad sectors), type the letter "Y" for "yes" and follow the screen prompts to insert a blank disk (if you are formatting the same disk, it is not necessary to insert another disk). If you do not wish to format another disk, type the letter "N" for "no."

6. Type N and then press <CR>

This will indicate that you do not want to format another disk. If you had just purchased a new box of disks, you probably would have indicated "Y" and then could have efficiently formatted each of the disks in the box.

7. End of this guided activity. Continue on to the next section.

GUIDED ACTIVITY: DO ANOTHER DIRECTORY OF YOUR BLANK DISK

1. Type **DIR A:**

    [*If you are using a floppy drive system type* **DIR B:**]

2. Press <CR>

The screen will appear similar to Figure 5-3. Now that the disk is formatted, the operating system can read the disk. The message "File not found" simply means that your disk is blank and contains no files.

```
d>DIR d:

  Volume in drive d has no label
  Directory of B:\

  File not found
```

Figure 5-3, Directory of Formatted Disk with No Files

3. End of this guided activity. Continue on to the next section.

BACKGROUND ON BACKING UP FILES

It is important to learn to backup your work. As discussed earlier, the disks are very susceptible to damage. When you backup, you copy your data from one disk to another so that you will have at least two disks with the same information on them. If one disk becomes unusable, you will still have at least one other disk that can be used. A file can be backed by using the **Copy** command.

Important note on copyright infringement: It is very important to understand that when we discuss "copying" a disk, we are discussing copying YOUR data disk, not licensed, copyrighted program disks. The majority of the application software (as well as the operating system programs) are protected by copyright laws. The only copies you may make of those types of disks are directed by the license agreement between the software publisher and the legal owner of the software program. The software user does not purchase the program, only the rights to use the program in accordance with the license agreement. Sometimes that license agreement will allow the user to make backup(s) of the original program disks as insurance against disk failures. This does not mean that the user can sell or give copies of the program to friends, colleagues, acquaintances, or strangers. The technology allows us to make copies of the copyrighted programs but the law does not allow it.

In the following activities, you will be copying a single file, groups of files that have either something in the filename or the extension in common, and finally, all of the files on a disk. The Copy command you will use is an internal command...that means that it is loaded into the microcomputer system when you load DOS. It remains in the system's memory until you turn off the system and is therefore available to you even when you remove the DOS program disk from the drive on the floppy system.

The Copy command allows you to transfer a copy of one or more files from one disk (or subdirectory--more on subdirectories later) to another without erasing any of the files located on the disk or subdirectory to which and from which you are copying. This is one method that can be used to backup your data files.

The Copy command will also allow you to rename the file you are copying so that when it is copied to the target, it will have a new name (the original file will still have the original name). Later on you will learn about the Rename command which offers a similar outcome but results in having only the original file on the disk with a new name. (We will work with the Rename command in the next unit.)

BACKGROUND ON SOURCE DISK DRIVE AND TARGET DISK DRIVE

For the remainder of the training presented in this book, you will be doing things that will help you to manage your disks and your files. In some of the activities you will be copying files from a disk. The disk that you copy from is referred to as the **source** disk. The disk that you copy to is referred to as the **target** disk. Where each of those disks is located will depend upon the system you are using.

If you are using a **hard disk system** the source drive could be drive A or drive C if you only have one floppy drive on the system. If the file(s) you want to copy are on the hard disk and you want to copy them to the floppy, drive C will be the source and drive A will be the target.

If you are using a *floppy disk system* the source drive could be drive A or drive B. If the file(s) you want to copy are on the disk in drive A and you want to copy them to the disk in drive B, drive A will be the source drive and drive B will be the target.

Regardless of the type of system you are using, the SOURCE drive and filespec information must always be specified first in the command and the TARGET information specified last.

In order to use the Copy command, the target disk must be formatted. The name of the file to be copied must be spelled correctly and the command must include the complete filespec (drive designation [if not the default drive], filename, and any extension).

GUIDED ACTIVITY: COPY A SINGLE FILE

1. Make sure that DOS is loaded and that the DOS prompt is displayed.

2. If you are using a hard disk system, the **Understanding and Using MS-DOS/PC DOS** training disk files must be available.

    [If you are using a floppy drive system, REMOVE THE DOS DISK from drive A and insert the Understanding and Using MS-DOS/PC DOS training disk into drive A.]

3. Your formatted data disk should be in the data drive (drive A for hard disk systems and *drive B if you are using a floppy disk drive system*).

4. Type **DIR/W** and then press **<CR>**

    You used the /W variation of the directory command because you only wanted to display the filenames from the **Understanding and Using MS-DOS/PC DOS** training disk and did not need the extra information provided by the DIR command. You did not have to type the drive specification because you want to display a directory from the default drive. The directory should look similar to Figure 5-4.

5. Look at Figure 5-4 and/or the screen display of the directory.

    Notice the file called **PROG.FIL**. That is the name of the file that you are going to copy.

6. Type **COPY C:PROG.FIL A:**

    [If you are using a floppy drive system type COPY A:PROG.FIL B:]

    Since a new filename is not specified, DOS will assume you want the filename to stay the same when it's copied to the target disk.

7. Press **<CR>**

    The command will execute, the file will copy, and a message will appear telling you "1 File(s) copied."

    If the system cannot find the specified file(s), it will indicate "0 File(s) Copied." If you get this message, check the spelling of the filename. Be sure you have included an extension if an extension was assigned to the filename (and in this activity you do have the .fil extension).

    If you receive the error message "Invalid # of Parameters" or "File cannot be copied onto itself", you might have made a mistake when you specified either your source or your target disk. Make sure that you specified the source disk and the target disk correctly.

If you made a mistake in typing the command, just retype it at the DOS prompt as described previously.

```
d>DIR/W
   Volume in drive d has no label
   Directory of d:\

      1AR          WKS  CALENDAR BAS  2AR          WKS  BANK         BAS  MENU         BAS
      AUTOEXEC BAT      3AR          WKS  AVERAGES BAS  TIME         BAS  WONDERS      BAS
      AUTOEXEC BAS      2SIDEDSK          ORDER        BAS  SQUARE       BAS  FIBONACI     BAS
      BOOT              MELLOW       BAS  CONFIG            DEFAULT           CPU
      COLDBOOT          EXTERNAL          BYTE              FILENAME          RESET
      DIR               FILE              EXT               BACKUP            COPY
      COMPUTER BAS      PROG         FIL  DATABASE FIL  DOCUMENT FIL  COPY         1
      COPY         2    COPY         3    AR1          WKS  AR2          WKS  AR3          WKS
      FILE1        PIC  FILE2        PIC  FILE3        PIC  AR1          PIC  AR2          PIC
      AR3          PIC  1AR          WK1  2AR          WK1  3AR          WK1  AR1          WK1
      AR2          WK1  AR3          WK1  NEWABC       DBF  NEWABC       DBT  ABC1         DBF
      ABC1         DBT  BLAIRLIN     DOC  LIB          DOC  LEASE        KEY  MEMO1
      MEMO2             MEMO3
           62 File(s)    260096 bytes free
```

Figure 5-4, Wide Directory of **Understanding and Using MS-DOS/PC DOS** Training Disk (The filenames may appear in a different order on your screen.)

8. Do a directory of your disk.

✔**CHECKPOINT**

How many files are on your disk now? _____

9. End of this guided activity. Continue on to the next section.

✱ BACKGROUND ON USING THE "WILDCARD" OR "GLOBAL" CHARACTERS WITH THE COPY COMMAND

When you wish to copy more than one file and there is some common element in the names of the files you wish to copy, you can use the **global** character (*) or the **wildcard** (?) to expedite the process. Sometimes you will see both the asterisk (*) and the question mark (?) referred to as wildcards, however, in this book we will refer to the question mark as a wildcard and the asterisk as a global character. The global character (*) tells DOS to stop reading at the point where the asterisk is typed and accept anything.

The wildcard (?), on the other hand, is a one character substitution. It tells DOS to accept any one character at the location where it is typed in the filename. For example, if you had files with the names **tip.dbf, tap.dbf, top.dbf**, you could copy them with one command by using the wildcard character -- COPY T?P.DBF *d:* -- in place of the middle letter of the filename. In the following guided activities, you will be copying multiple files using the global character and the wildcard.

BACKGROUND ON COPYING FILES THAT HAVE A COMMON EXTENSION USING THE GLOBAL CHARACTER (*)

Look at Figure 5-4. Notice three files: **DATABASE.FIL, DOCUMENT.FIL,** and **PROG.FIL.** These files all have the same extension, **FIL,** in common. By using the global character, you will be able to copy all three files with only one command. You will type the asterisk where the filename should appear. This will tell DOS to accept any character(s) at the point where the asterisk (*) is typed. When DOS reads the period that separates the filename from its extension, it will start to read again. You will type .FIL to tell DOS that you want only files that have .FIL as an extension.

GUIDED ACTIVITY: COPY FILES THAT HAVE A COMMON EXTENSION USING GLOBAL CHARACTER (*)

1. Make sure that DOS is loaded and that the system prompt is displayed.

   If you are using a hard disk system, the **Understanding and Using MS-DOS/PC DOS** training disk files must be available.

   *[If you are using a floppy drive system, the **Understanding and Using MS-DOS/PC DOS** training disk should be in drive A.]*

   Your formatted data disk should be in the data drive (drive A for hard disk systems and *drive B if you are using a floppy disk drive system*).

2. Type **COPY C:*.FIL A:**

   *[If you are using a floppy drive system type **COPY A:*.FIL B:**]*

   This command tells the system that you want to copy from the source disk (drive C if using a hard disk system and *drive A if using a floppy disk system*) to the target disk (drive A if using a hard disk system and *drive B if using a floppy disk system*) any file that has a **.FIL** extension and that you don't care what filename is to the left of that extension. We specified the default drive for purposes of clarity, even though it is not necessary to specify the default drive in a command.

3. Press **<CR>**

   The command will be executed and the name of each of the files that is copied will appear on the screen as it is copied. When the copying process is complete, the system will let you know that "3 File(s) copied" and the DOS prompt will be the last thing on the screen.

   If the system cannot find the files, it will indicate "0 File(s) copied." If you should get this message, check the spelling of the filename and extension.

   If you receive the error message "Invalid # of Parameters" or "File cannot be copied onto itself", you might have made a mistake when you specified either your source or your target disk. Make sure that you specified the source disk and the target disk correctly. If you made a mistake in typing the command, just retype it at the DOS prompt as described previously.

4. Do a directory of your disk.

✔CHECKPOINT

How many files are on your disk now? _____ 3 _____

5. End of this guided activity. Continue on to the next section.

BACKGROUND ON COPYING FILES THAT HAVE A COMMON FILENAME BY USING THE GLOBAL (*) CHARACTER

As we mentioned earlier, when you wish to copy more than one file and there is some common element in the names of the files you wish to copy, you can use the global character to expedite the process. In the following guided activity, you will be copying multiple files that have the same filename by including the global character in place of the extension.

Look at Figure 5-4. Notice that four files: **COPY, COPY.1, COPY.2,** and **COPY.3** all have the same filename (**COPY**) in common. By using the global character, you will be able to copy all four files with only one command.

GUIDED ACTIVITY: COPY FILES THAT HAVE A COMMON FILENAME BY USING THE GLOBAL (*) CHARACTER

1. Make sure that DOS is loaded and that the system prompt is displayed.

   If you are using a hard disk system, the **Understanding and Using MS-DOS/PC DOS** training disk files must be available.

   *[If you are using a floppy drive system, the **Understanding and Using MS-DOS/PC DOS** training disk should be in drive A.]*

   Your formatted data disk should be in the data drive (drive A for hard disk systems and *drive B if you are using a floppy disk drive system*).

2. Type COPY C:COPY.* A:

   [If you are using a floppy drive system type COPY A:COPY. B:]*

   This command tells the system that you want to copy all the files from the source disk to the target disk that have **COPY** as the filename. The extension can be anything. We specified the default drive for purposes of clarity even though it is not necessary to specify the default drive in a command.

3. Press **<CR>**

   The command will be executed and the name of each of the files that is copied will appear on the screen as it is copied. When the copying process is complete, the system will let you know that "4 File(s) copied" and the DOS prompt will be the last thing on the screen.

If the system cannot find the files, it will indicate "0 File(s) copied." If you should get this message, check the spelling of the filename and extension.

If you receive the error message "Invalid # of Parameters" or "File cannot be copied onto itself", you might have made a mistake when you specified either your source or your target disk. Make sure that you specified the source disk and the target disk correctly. If you made a mistake in typing the command, just retype it at the DOS prompt as described previously.

4. Do a directory of your disk.

✔CHECKPOINT

How many files are on your disk now? ___7___

5. End of this guided activity. Continue on to the next section.

GUIDED ACTIVITY: COPY FILES USING THE WILDCARD (?) CHARACTER AS A SUBSTITUTION FOR ONE CHARACTER IN A FILENAME

You are going to copy the 1AR.WKS, 3AR.WKS, 2AR.WKS files. You will use the wildcard character to stand in for the first character in the filename so that DOS will accept any character as the first character.

1. Make sure that DOS is loaded and that the system prompt is displayed.

   If you are using a hard disk system, the **Understanding and Using MS-DOS/PC DOS** training disk files must be available.

   *[If you are using a floppy drive system, the **Understanding and Using MS-DOS/PC DOS** training disk should be in drive A.*]

   Your formatted data disk should be in the data drive (drive A for hard disk systems and *drive B if you are using a floppy disk drive system*).

2. Type **COPY C:?AR.WKS A:**

   *[If you are using a floppy drive system type **COPY A:?AR.WKS B:**]*

3. Press **<CR>**

   The command tells DOS to copy all the files that have names begining with any character and then *AR* and that have a *.WKS* extension.

4. Do a directory of your disk.

✔CHECKPOINT

How many files are on your disk now? ____10 × 13____

5. End of this guided activity. Continue on to the next section.

BACKGROUND ON COPYING ALL OF THE FILES ON A DISK USING DISKCOPY VERSUS THE COPY FILE-BY-FILE COMMAND

One of the commands that you can use to copy all of the files on a disk is the **Copy file-by-file** command. Another command that can be used to copy the entire contents of one floppy disk onto another is the **Diskcopy** command. A third command that you could use if you are using DOS version 3.2 or later is called the **Xcopy** command (we'll use that one in the next unit). Right now we'll just provide a short explanation of the **Copy file-by-file** command and the **Diskcopy** command.

Copy File-by-File Command

The **Copy file-by-file** command must be used with a disk that is already formatted. It will copy all of the files from the source disk to the target disk. Files already on the target disk as well as those on the source disk will not be erased. If there is not enough room for all of the files to copy from the source disk, the files that the target disk can store will copy and then you will receive a message that there is no more room on the disk.

When the system stores a file, it doesn't store it in one big clump on one spot of a disk. Rather, it takes the pieces of a file and puts those pieces in the first available spots it finds. The storage spots may not always be in the same vicinity on the disk. Over time, as a file is manipulated, it tends to become "fragmented." In other words, each time a file is retrieved and edited and saved to the disk, the little pieces of the file are scattered all around the disk. The system always knows where the pieces can be located (unless the disk becomes damaged in some way); but, the more fragmented the file is, the longer it will take the system to pull all the pieces together in order to present you with the complete file. Obviously, this decreases its efficiency.

When a file is copied using the Copy file-by-file command, it is pulled back together and stored sequentially on the disk so that the system can access the file in an efficient fashion. Using this technique can improve performance with a floppy disk. (Note: the same type of slowdown can develop on a hard disk but there are other ways to regain its peak performance; however, those methods are beyond the scope of this book.)

The Diskcopy Command

If you need to make several copies of a data disk and have a box of unformatted disks, you might decide to use the Copy file-by-file command to make the first copy onto a blank, formatted disk. Once you make the "master copy," you can then use the Diskcopy command to make the remaining copies without having to format the new disks. The Diskcopy command will format a disk and then copy the entire contents of a disk onto another disk. The Diskcopy command differs from the Copy file-by-file command in several respects.

The Diskcopy command will format a disk before it makes the copy. It will, therefore, erase any files that may be stored on the target disk. The diskcopy command will make a mirror image of the disk that is being copied; if a file is fragmented on the source disk, it will still be fragmented after it has been copied to the target disk using the Diskcopy command.

The Diskcopy command is not suitable for copying to or from a hard disk. If you should use it on a hard disk system, DOS will assume that you are copying from one floppy disk to another and so will prompt you to insert the disks as appropriate (first source then target then source and so on).

Once in a while, it may be necessary for you to copy a disk that has hidden files. Hidden files are files that are stored on a disk even though their filenames are not displayed on a disk's directory. There are hidden files on the DOS disk. When you want to make a backup copy of the DOS disk, you must use the Diskcopy command in order to get a copy that works because Copy file-by-file doesn't copy the hidden files.

Diskcopy is an external command so the DOS program files must be available when you attempt to issue the command. Remember, the Copy command is an internal command so that program instructions for that command are stored in the system's memory when DOS is loaded.

GUIDED ACTIVITY: COPY FILE-BY-FILE

You are now going to copy all the files from the **Understanding and Using MS-DOS/PC DOS** training disk to your data disk. If you are using a hard disk system, we are sure that it has been set up so that when you do this copy, only the files that are from the training disk will be copied because you should be working in a subdirectory containing only those files. (This is a topic we will cover in Unit 7.)

1. Make sure that DOS is loaded and that the system prompt is displayed.

    If you are using a hard disk system, the **Understanding and Using MS-DOS/PC DOS** training disk files must be available.

    *[If you are using a floppy drive system, the **Understanding and Using MS-DOS/PC DOS** training disk should be in drive A.]*

    Your formatted data disk should be in the data drive (drive A for hard disk systems and *drive B if you are using a floppy disk drive system*).

2. Type **COPY C:*.* A:**

    *[If you are using a floppy drive system type **COPY A:*.* B:**]*

    The first drive reference is to the source disk (the disk you are copying from). The second drive reference refers to the target disk (the disk you are copying to). The first global character (*) tells DOS to copy any filename and the second global character tells DOS to copy any extension...therefore, all files will be copied.

3. Press **<CR>**

    The command will be executed and the filenames will appear on the screen as they are being copied. If you made a mistake in typing the command, just retype it at the DOS prompt as described previously.

4. End of this guided activity. Continue on to the next section.

A LITTLE MORE BACKGROUND ON THIS COPYING BUSINESS

In the previous guided activity, you might have noticed that you copied several files more than one time. For example, you copied the file **Prog.fil** in two separate guided activities. Then, when you did the Copy file-by-file, you copied the file again. What do you think happened? Was the file copied for the third time when you issued the Copy file-by-file command?

Yes, the file was copied all three times. You saw the filename displayed on the screen as it was copied along with the other files that were being copied. Does the filename appear more than one time on the disk? What is the easiest way to find out?

That's right, display a directory of the target disk. When you do the directory, you will see that the filename **Prog.fil** appears only once on the disk. The **Prog.fil** appeared once when you made the first copy. Then, when you copied all the .FIL files, the file copied a second time, and finally copied a third time when you did the Copy file-by-file. Each time it was copied, the new copy overwrote the previous copy. This is known as "updating" a file. We normally don't say "never" but we'll go out on a limb this time. You will <u>never</u> see the same filename with the same extension in the same directory on the same disk.

REVIEW QUESTIONS

Know Formatting from what to what

1. Is it acceptable to put a space in a filename when using it in a command?

    NO

2. You are using a floppy drive system and put a brand new disk into drive B and type the DIR command. You receive the message "Disk error reading drive B, Abort, Retry, Ignore?" After you abort the request, what command can you use to prepare the disk so that it can be read by the system? In your answer, indicate which disk should be in drive A and which disk should be in drive B. Write the command exactly as you would type it.

    drive A - DOS disk
    drive B - blank disk   *DIR B: x Format B: ↵*

3. You need a disk for a new project you are starting. You grab a disk and format it. You then realize that the disk you just formatted had an important report stored on it. What happened to the report?   *It was erased.*

4. The disk in drive A has a file named "Benefits.doc" stored on it. You wish to copy it to the hard disk (drive C). DOS is loaded and the C> is on the screen with the cursor blinking next to it. Write the command exactly as you would type it to accomplish the task.

    COPY A: Benefits.doc-B   Copy A: Benefits.doc B

5. DOS is loaded and the A> is on the screen. The disk in drive B has some files that you wish to copy--**Unit.1   Unit.2   Unit.3**--along with some files that you do not want to copy. Write the command that would allow you to copy all of the specified files to the formatted disk in drive A with just one command.

    A)   COPY B: unit. B: then enter*

    source target

f/m

6. You have a formatted disk in drive B that has one file on it that you want to keep. You want to copy all the files from the disk in drive A to the disk in drive B. Write the command you would use exactly as you would type it. DOS is loaded and the A> is on the screen.

COPY A:*.* _B:
              space

DOCUMENTATION RESEARCH

1. The copy command can copy a file to the same disk. Since you can't have two files on the same disk with the same name, how can the copy command accomplish that task?

2. What will happen if you use the global character in a filename when you are using the Type command?

3. If you specify the /S switch in the Format command, what files are copied from the default drive to the target drive?

4. When you format a disk with the /V switch, is the volume label subject to all of the same restrictions as filenames? If not, how do they differ?

5. What will the following command accomplish? FORMAT B: /S

6. When DOS is used to format a disk, one of the things it does is create a File Allocation Table (FAT). How does the DOS documentation describe this area?

UNIT
6
ADDITIONAL DOS COMMANDS FOR FILE AND DISK MANAGEMENT

SUPPLIES NEEDED

In order to complete this unit, you will need:

1. this book;
2. DOS command program files;
3. the **Understanding and Using MS-DOS/PC DOS** training disk files;
4. your data disk.

OBJECTIVES

After completing this unit you will be able to:

1. rename a file;
2. delete a file;
3. delete more than one file;
4. define memory;
5. use the Checkdisk command;
6. use the Xcopy command;
7. use the Type command;
8. format a disk with the system on it;
9. format a disk with a volume label.

d – is designated drive

IMPORTANT KEYSTROKES AND COMMANDS

The important keystrokes and commands that will be introduced in this unit are:
Note: **d** = designated drive   **filename** = name of file   **ext** = name of extension

1. Rename a file . . . . Ren d:oldname.ext newname.ext
2. Delete a file from disk . . . . Del d:filename.ext
3. Delete files with same filename . . . . Del d:filename.*

75

 4. Delete files with same extension . . . . Del d:*.ext
 5. Check a disk . . . . Chkdsk d:
 6. Xcopy files with same filename . . . . Xcopy d:filename.* d:
 7. Xcopy files with same extension . . . . Xcopy d:*.ext d:
 8. Xcopy all files . . . . Xcopy d:*.* d:
 9. Type the contents of a file . . . . Type d:filename.ext
10. Format a disk with the system . . . . Format d: /s
11. Format a disk with a volume label . . . . Format d: /v

ASSIGNMENTS

1. _____   Review Questions
2. _____   Documentation Research

BACKGROUND ON RENAMING A FILE USING THE RENAME COMMAND

Sometimes it is necessary to rename a file. You might think of a more descriptive name or perhaps you realize you assigned an inaccurate description to a file. One solution for this type of problem is to use the rename command. For example, let's assume that you named a file SMITH when it really should have been named JONES. The disk with the SMITH file is in drive A. You would use this command to rename the SMITH file:

REN A:SMITH JONES

This command results in having the name of the SMITH file changed to JONES. Nothing has been changed in the contents of the file, only its name. The command does not generate a new file, SMITH simply does not exist...he changed his name to JONES.

GUIDED ACTIVITY: RENAME A FILE USING THE RENAME COMMAND

You are going to use the Rename command to change the name of the COPY file that is on your data disk.

1. Make sure that DOS is loaded and that the system prompt is displayed.

2. If you are using a hard disk system, the DOS command program files should be available.

   [If you are using a floppy drive system, the DOS disk should be in drive A]

3. Your formatted data disk that now contains all the files from the **Understanding and Using MS-DOS/PC DOS** training disk should be in the data drive (drive A for hard disk systems and *drive B if you are using a floppy disk drive system*).

4. Type **DIR A: /W**

   *[If you are using a floppy drive system type **DIR B: /W**]*

5. Press **<CR>**

A directory similar to the one shown in Figure 6-1 should appear.

Look at the directory. You should see a file named COPY. It has no extension. You are going to change that filename so that it has an extension. The new name will be COPY.4 (that way it will match the other COPY files that we have on the disk).

```
d>DIR/W
   Volume in drive d has no label
   Directory of d:\

1AR          WKS   CALENDAR  BAS   2AR        WKS   BANK      BAS   MENU      BAS
AUTOEXEC BAT       3AR       WKS   AVERAGES   BAS   TIME      BAS   WONDERS   BAS
AUTOEXEC BAS       2SIDEDSK        ORDER      BAS   SQUARE    BAS   FIBONACI  BAS
BOOT               MELLOW    BAS   CONFIG           DEFAULT         CPU
COLDBOOT           EXTERNAL        BYTE             FILENAME        RESET
DIR                FILE            EXT              BACKUP          COPY
COMPUTER BAS       PROG      FIL   DATABASE   FIL   DOCUMENT  FIL   COPY      1
COPY     2         COPY      3     AR1        WKS   AR2       WKS   AR3       WKS
FILE1    PIC       FILE2     PIC   FILE3      PIC   AR1       PIC   AR2       PIC
AR3      PIC       1AR       WK1   2AR        WK1   3AR       WK1   AR1       WK1
AR2      WK1       AR3       WK1   NEWABC     DBF   NEWABC    DBT   ABC1      DBF
ABC1     DBT       BLAIRLIN  DOC   LIB        DOC   LEASE     KEY   MEMO1
MEMO2              MEMO3
      62 File(s)   260096 bytes free
```

Figure 6-1, Directory of Your Data Disk

6. Type **REN A:COPY COPY.4**

   [*If you are using a floppy drive system type* **REN B:COPY COPY.4**]

   You are telling the system to go to the designated disk and rename the file currently called "Copy" to "Copy.4". Be sure to type the current filename and then leave a blank space before typing the file's new name. Do not repeat the drive designation for the new name. DOS assumes that you want the renaming done on the same disk. If you include a drive letter for the new name, most version of DOS will give you an error message.

7. Press **<CR>**

   The light on the drive that you specified in the command will turn on. The file will be renamed. The command does not provide a message when it is through. The DOS prompt simply reappears on the screen. If something is wrong with the command or if the system cannot find the specified file, it will give you a message. You can assume a "no news is good news" response if the command is successful. Or, you can assume a "show me" attitude, and display a directory of you data disk that shows only files with the name COPY.

✔CHECKPOINT

a. You have decided to adopt the "show me" attitude. Write the command that will display a directory of your data disk that includes only files with the filename "COPY" and any extension.

DIR A: COPY.*

8. Do a directory of your data disk. Display only files with the filename "COPY". Any extension is acceptable.

✔ CHECKPOINT

b. Look at the directory you have just displayed. Is the COPY filename displayed on the directory? Is the COPY.4 filename displayed?

_____

The COPY.4 file is the same as the file that was previously named COPY. Only the names have been changed, not the file's contents.

9. End of this guided activity. Continue on to the next section.

BACKGROUND ON RENAMING A FILE USING THE COPY COMMAND

There may be times when you want to store two versions of the same file on the same disk in the same directory. Since DOS does not permit you to use two identical filenames on a disk in the same directory, you must store the file using two different filenames. One approach you might take is to use the Copy command to copy the original version of the file from a disk to the same disk. When you do this, you must be sure to give the target file a different name. For example, if you have a file named CONTRACT1 and you would like another copy of that file so that you could make some changes to it, you could use the following command. (Assume that your data disk is in drive A.)

COPY A:CONTRACT1 A:CONTRACT2

This command results in having the original CONTRACT1 file on the disk in drive A and an identical copy of that file also on the disk in drive A with the name "CONTRACT2." If this is a file that you use with your word processor, you could then use the word processing program to edit CONTRACT2 without disturbing the contents of CONTRACT1.

GUIDED ACTIVITY: COPY FILE TO SAME DISK WITH NEW NAME

If you look at Figure 6-1 you will see a filename "MENU.BAS". Let's assume you know how to write programs in Basica and you want to create a menu similar to MENU.BAS, yet keep the orignal MENU.BAS as it is. What you need is a copy of the file so that you can make the changes without modifying the original program file. You want both files on the same disk.

1. Make sure that DOS is loaded and that the system prompt is displayed.

2. If you are using a hard disk system, the DOS command program files must be available.

   [If you are using a floppy drive system, the DOS disk should be in drive A]

3. Your data disk with the files copied from the **Understanding and Using MS-DOS/PC DOS** training disk should be in the data drive (drive A for hard disk systems and _drive B if you are using a floppy disk drive system_).

You are going to copy **from** your data disk **to** your data disk.

4. Type **COPY A:MENU.BAS A:MENU2.BAS**

    [*If you are using a floppy drive system type* **COPY B:MENU.BAS B:MENU2.BAS**]

5. Press **<CR>**

    The copy will be made. Time to take a look at the directory listing for your data disk.

6. Do a directory of your data disk. Do you see MENU.BAS? Do you see MENU2.BAS? *DIR B:*

    Both files should be on your data disk. Now, if you wanted to modify the MENU2.BAS file, you would have to know how to write programs in BASIC so you could pull up the MENU2.BAS file to modify it.

✔CHECKPOINT

c. You want to change the MENU.BAS filename so that it is more consistent with the MENU2.BAS filename. You want MENU.BAS to be named MENU1.BAS. Write the command that would make that change.

    Ren B:Menu.BAS Menu1.BAS

7. Enter the command that will change the **MENU.BAS** filename on your data disk to **MENU1.BAS**.

8. Do a directory listing only filenames that begin with "**MENU**". *DIR B:Menu **

✔CHECKPOINT

d. What command did you type?

    *DIR B: Menu *.* *

9. End of this guided activity. Continue on to the next section.

BACKGROUND ON DELETING (ERASING) A FILE

Sometimes you no longer need a file and so want to delete it. It is just as easy to delete or erase a file as it is to copy a file. Just as when you use the Copy command to copy one or more file(s), it is possible to delete a single file, delete several files, or delete all of the files on a disk by using the Delete (Erase) command with the global or wildcard characters if needed.

This is one of those commands where "no news is good news." If you do not receive an error message, you have issued the command correctly. Otherwise, you will receive an error message. In the following guided activity, you will first **Delete** a file and then you will **Erase** three files. We are just showing you that either of the two commands will accomplish the task of deleting a file(s).

We do not recommend that you use the Delete (erase) command to delete all of the files on a disk. If you want to delete all of the files on a disk, it is usually better to use the Format command because the Format command will let you know if there are any bad sectors on the disk and then set those bad sectors aside so that nothing will be stored on them.

GUIDED ACTIVITY: DELETE A FILE USING THE DELETE COMMAND

You are going to use the DEL (Delete) command to erase the COPY.1 file from your data disk.

1. Make sure that DOS is loaded and that the system prompt is displayed.

2. If you are using a hard disk system, the DOS command program files should be available.

   [If you are using a floppy drive system, the DOS disk should be in drive A]

3. Your formatted data disk with all the files copied from the **Understanding and Using MS-DOS/PC DOS** training disk should be in the data drive (drive A for hard disk systems and *drive B if you are using a floppy disk drive system*).

4. Type **DEL A:COPY.1**

   *[If you are using a floppy drive system type **DEL B:COPY.1**]*

5. Press **<CR>**

   The in-use light on the designated drive will come on and the command will execute. As stated earlier, however, you will not receive a message if the command executes properly. If the command does not execute properly, find the error in the command that you typed and then carefully retype it on the current line of the screen.

6. Type **DIR A:COPY.1**

   *[If you are using a floppy drive system type **DIR B:COPY.1**]*

7. Press **<CR>**

   You should receive a message saying "File not found" (because you deleted it).

8. End of this guided activity. Continue on to the next section.

GUIDED ACTIVITY: ERASE THREE FILES USING THE GLOBAL CHARACTER

You are going to use the ERASE command to delete all files that have .FIL as an extension. Since you are going to erase more than one file, it is a good idea to do a directory asking for those files so that you can be sure you are not about to erase something you will need later.

1. Make sure that DOS is loaded and that the system prompt is displayed.

2. If you are using a hard disk system, the DOS command program files should be available.

   [If you are using a floppy drive system, the DOS disk should be in drive A]

3. Your formatted data disk with the files that you copied from the **Understanding and Using MS-DOS/PC DOS** training disk should be in the data drive (drive A for hard disk systems and *drive B if you are using a floppy disk drive system*).

4. Type **DIR A:*.FIL**

    [*If you are using a floppy drive system type* **DIR B:*.FIL**]

5. Press **<CR>**

    A directory listing just those three files with the .FIL extension will be displayed on the screen. You can then check the filenames to be sure that you do want to erase them with the next command.

6. Type **ERASE A:*.FIL**

    [*If you are using a floppy drive system type* **ERASE B:*.FIL**]

7. Press **<CR>**

    The in-use light on the designated drive will come on and the command will execute. As stated earlier, however, you will not receive a message if the command executes properly. If the command does not execute properly, find the error in the command that you typed and then carefully retype it on the current line of the screen.

8. Display a directory of your data disk asking only for filenames with an .FIL extension.

    "File not found" should be your reward for a job well-done.

9. End of this guided activity. Continue on to the next section.

BACKGROUND ON MEMORY

Some new users have a hard time distinguishing between the number of bytes of random access memory in the system and the number of bytes of storage available on a disk. Sometimes the analogy of a desktop and file cabinets makes the difference between the two a little easier to understand.

The memory of a system might be built up in increments of 64K or 256K. You can think of memory in the computer as a desktop. If you have 64K memory, you have a very, very small desk and therefore don't have much space on which to work. In fact, in this day and age, with 64K you can't even load most application software (256K certainly can be considered minimal and 512K - 640K is definitely standard). (The explanation for the units of storage can be found in Unit 1, pages 11-12.)

If you have 640K or more of memory, you are much closer to having the electronic version of an executive's desk with lots of room to work. You can load powerful application software and still have plenty of room to pull your files out on your desk and manipulate them.

The amount of space available on disks is also measured in bytes. You can think of the bytes available on a disk as storage space, or the electronic equivalent of a file cabinet. If you have a single-sided, single density disk (becoming a rarity), you don't have much room in which to store your files (a little like a one-drawer file cabinet). Disks are available, however, in megabyte (millions of bytes) and even gigabyte (billions of bytes) capacities (a little like several multiple-drawer file cabinets).

You might be interested to find out how much space is available on the data disk you are using, how much of it is already being used by the files you have copied to the disk, and how much memory is available in the system you are using. The Checkdisk command will give you this type of information.

BACKGROUND ON CHECKDISK COMMAND

The Checkdisk command will report on how much total space is available on a disk, the number of files on a disk and the amount of space taken up by those files. It will also indicate the number of bytes (if any) in bad sectors, and the total amount of space free on a disk (which, of course, is really just the difference between the total space available on the disk and the amount of space taken up by the files and bad sectors). (Note: If a disk does have bad sectors, you may want to use the COPY *.* command or the XCOPY *.* command-- we'll use that one a little later--to copy all your files to another formatted disk).

The Checkdisk command also will provide you with a memory status report regarding the system you are using. It will state the total memory in the system and the amount of memory that is still available after any programs are laoded (loaded) (ex. DOS takes up space in the system's memory).

The Checkdisk command is an external command.

GUIDED ACTIVITY: USE CHECKDISK ON YOUR DATA DISK

1. Make sure that DOS is loaded and that the system prompt is displayed.

2. If you are using a hard disk system, the DOS command program files must be available.

   [If you are using a floppy drive system, the DOS DISK must be in drive A.]

3. Your data disk with the files copied from the **Understanding and Using MS-DOS/PC DOS** training disk should be in the data drive (drive A for hard disk systems and *drive B if you are using a floppy disk drive system*).

4. Type **CHKDSK A:**

   [*If you are using a floppy drive system type* **CHKDSK B:**]

5. Press **<CR>**

   If you receive a message "Bad command or filename" you should check the spelling in the command you typed; make sure the spacing is correct; and check to be sure that the drive designation is followed by a colon (not a semicolon). If all of this looks correct and you still get the same message, check to be sure that the DOS files are available to you on the hard disk you are using (ask the lab assistant or your instructor). *If you are using a floppy system, double check to be sure that the DOS disk is in drive A.* Remember, CHKDSK is an external command.

✔CHECKPOINT

e.   What is an external command?   How are they different from internal commands?

It is a command put in by the user. They are not in the main memory.

6.   If you did get an error message, correct the error and repeat the command as shown in steps 4 and 5.

If the command worked correctly, you should see something similar to Figure 6-2 on your screen.

```
d>CHKDSK d:

    362496 bytes total disk space
     77824 bytes in 59 user files
    282624 bytes available on disk

    655360 bytes total memory        (this section gives info about the system you are using,
    594400 bytes free                not about your data disk)
```

Figure 6-2, Sample of Statistics Generated by Checkdisk Command

✔CHECKPOINT

f.   How many bytes of total disk space do you have?_____

g.   How many bytes are used by user files?   _____

h.   How many bytes are available on the disk?   _____

i.   Does the disk have any bad sectors?   _____

j.   How much memory is in the system?   _____

k.   How much of the system's memory is available?   _____

7.   End of this guided activity.   Continue on to the next section.

BACKGROUND ON THE TYPE COMMAND

The **Type** command can sometimes be used to display the contents of a file if that file is stored as an ASCII file.   ASCII is the acronym for American Standard Code for Information Exchange.   At this point in your training, you don't need to be concerned with ASCII code except to realize that if you use the **Type** command and the file contents appear to be garbled and consist of strange symbols, the file is not stored as an ASCII file.   You will use the Type command to display the contents of both a file that is stored as an ASCII file and one that is not. (Please note, if a file is not stored as an ASCII, it may be possible to convert it to ASCII. That subject is beyond the scope of this introductory book, but you should be aware of the possibilities. You may learn more about this when you learn to use application software or if you should decide to learn programming.)

Type is an internal command.

GUIDED ACTIVITY: USE TYPE COMMAND TO DISPLAY CONTENTS OF FILE STORED AS AN ASCII FILE

You are going to use the Type command to display the contents of a file stored on your data disk. The file is creatively named FILE.

1. Make sure that DOS is loaded and that the system prompt is displayed.

2. If you are using a hard disk system, the DOS command program files should be available.

    [If you are using a floppy drive system, the DOS disk can be in drive A.]

3. Your data disk with the **Understanding and Using MS-DOS/PC DOS** training files should be in the data drive (drive A for hard disk systems and *drive B if you are using a floppy disk drive system*).

4. Type **TYPE A:FILE**

    *[If you are using a floppy drive system type **TYPE B:FILE**]*

5. Press **<CR>**

    The contents of the file will be displayed and will look like Figure 6-3.

```
d>TYPE d:FILE

    File:  Related data.  Any data with which you work is stored in
    the form of a file.  Examples of files include word processing
    documents, data bases, spreadsheets, programs, and graphs.
```

Figure 6-3, Results of the Type Command Using File Named "FILE"

6. End of this guided activity. Continue on to the next section.

GUIDED ACTIVITY: USE TYPE COMMAND TO DISPLAY CONTENTS OF FILE NOT STORED AS ASCII

You are now going to attempt to display the contents of a file that is not stored as an ASCII file. You have used this file before...remember CALENDAR.BAS.

1. Make sure that DOS is loaded and that the system prompt is displayed.

2. If you are using a hard disk system, the DOS files should be available.

   [If you are using a floppy drive system, the DOS disk can be in drive A.]

3. Your data disk with the **Understanding and Using MS-DOS/PC DOS** training files should be in the data drive (drive A for hard disk systems and *drive B if you are using a floppy disk drive system*).

4. Type **TYPE A:CALENDAR.BAS**

   *[If you are using a floppy drive system type **TYPE B:CALENDAR.BAS**]*

5. Press **<CR>**

   Whoops!?! The computer beeped at you a few times and then displayed something that looks kind of interesting and vaguely familiar; but, it sure doesn't look exactly like the CALENDAR.BAS file that you listed earlier in your training, does it? This file is <u>not</u> stored as an ASCII file and therefore you see some strange little symbols on your screen.

6. End of this guided activity. Continue on to the next section.

BACKGROUND ON FORMATTING A DISK WITH THE SYSTEM

Earlier in your training session, you formatted your new disk so that the system could read from and write to the disk. When we discussed formatting, we also said that formatting was a good way to erase a disk.

You are at the point in your training where you need to erase the entire contents of your data disk so that you will be ready to begin a new project. When you format this time, you are going to indicate that you want to format the disk with the system on it by using the /S switch.

If you format a disk with the system on it, it means that you will be able to load that disk as well as use the DOS internal commands. You might want to format a disk with the system on it to use for storing programs. Then, you won't have to use a separate disk to load DOS first and then the program. This type of disk is said to be **self-loading (self-booting)**.

Disks that don't have the system on them can only store data and are not self-loading, but they have more room to store data files.

Remember that the Format command is an external command.

GUIDED ACTIVITY: FORMAT DISK WITH SYSTEM

1. Make sure that DOS is loaded and that the system prompt is displayed.

2. If you are using a hard disk system, the DOS command program files must be available.

   [If you are using a floppy drive system, the DOS DISK must be in drive A.]

3. Your data disk with all the files you've copied from the **Understanding and Using MS-DOS/PC DOS** training disk should be in the data drive (drive A for hard disk systems and *drive B if you are using a floppy disk drive system*).

4. Type **FORMAT A: /S**

   [*If you are using a floppy drive system type* **FORMAT B: /S**]

5. Press **<CR>**

   When the system prompts you to insert a new disk in the designated drive, make sure that the disk you wish to format is in the designated drive. Depending on which version of DOS you are using, the system will either prompt you to press "any key" or to press "RETURN" to continue.

6. Press the appropriate key to begin the formatting process.

   A message may appear on the screen indicating a head and cylinder count or that the system is "Formatting..." and the in-use light on the specified drive will be on.

```
            Formatting...Format complete
            System Transferred

            xxxxxx bytes total disk space
             xxxxx bytes used by system
            xxxxxx bytes available on disk


            Format another (Y/N)? ____
```

Figure 6-4, Format Completion Message after Format with System

   When the formatting process is complete, a message similar to the one illustrated in Figure 6-4 will appear and you will be asked if you wish to format another disk. If you wish to format another disk, type the letter "Y" for "yes" and follow the screen prompts to insert a blank disk. If you do not wish to format another disk, type the letter "N" for "no."

7. Type N and then press **<CR>**

8. Display a wide directory of your data disk.

   The directory should list one file, COMMAND.COM. This disk is now ready to store files. As a result of the Format /S command, your data disk is "self-loading." You could put it into Drive A and do a warm boot and the system would be able to load DOS (the internal commands for DOS are stored in the COMMAND.COM file that is listed on your disk's directory).

9. End of this guided activity. Continue on to the next section.

BACKGROUND ON THE XCOPY COMMAND

The DOS **Xcopy** command was first introduced in DOS 3.2. **Xcopy** is an external command that provides a faster method to copy groups of files offering more options than the ordinary Copy command. **Xcopy** will copy files, directories, and subdirectories (which we remind you will be covered in Unit 7 of this book). The Copy command will not copy directories and subdirectories.

Xcopy performs its copying routine with fewer disk accesses than the Copy command. If you will remember, when you did the copying in the previous guided activities, DOS first searched the source disk for the file you asked to copy and then made the copy onto the target disk. If there was more than one file, DOS had to go back to the source disk each time it was ready to copy another file. When you use the **Xcopy** command, you will observe a slightly different routine. DOS will read as many files as possible into the system's memory (so it does all its reading from the source disk at one time). Then, DOS writes a copy of each of the files to the target disk. This method cuts down on the number of times DOS must access each disk which increases copying efficiency and speed.

You can use the same types of parameters with **Xcopy** as you did with the Copy command including the use of the global or wildcard characters. **Xcopy** offers additional parameters (or switches). As mentioned previously, you can specify that you want to include subdirectories in the copy (/e). You can also specify that you only want files modified on or after a specified date (/d switch). The /v switch will verify each file as it is written to the target and the /w switch will cause **Xcopy** to wait before it starts copying files (this is the only switch that we will use in your training and it only needs to be used with a floppy disk system). This command offers a lot of flexibility and should be explored further. However, we only intend to introduce you to its existence in this training. As you need the flexibility of the command, you can use the DOS documentation to take advantage of Xcopy's other switches.

Remember, this is an external command so the DOS program files must be available. If you are using a hard disk, the system should be set up so that these files can be found (check with the lab assistant or your instructor if you have problems accessing the external DOS commands). If you are using a *floppy drive system, the DOS program disk must be in drive A.*

GUIDED ACTIVITY: USE THE XCOPY COMMAND TO COPY
ALL FILES WITH A .PIC EXTENSION

You have plenty of space on your data disk. Let's do a little work with **Xcopy** to fill up some of that space. You are going to copy all the files that have .PIC as an extension to your data disk.

You will use the /W switch because some of you are using a floppy disk system. You will need the pause that the /W provides so that you can switch disks before the copying process begins. Those of you using hard disk systems will not have to switch disks because the files you want to copy as well as the external DOS commands are all available on the hard disk.

1. Make sure that DOS is loaded and that the system prompt is displayed.

2. If you are using a hard disk system, the **Understanding and Using MS-DOS/PC DOS** training disk files as well as the DOS command program files must be available.

[If you are using a floppy drive system, you must start this activity with the DOS disk in drive A. You will be instructed when to remove the DOS disk from drive A and insert the **Understanding and Using MS-DOS/PC DOS** *training disk into drive A.]*

3. Your formatted data disk should be in the data drive (drive A for hard disk systems and *drive B if you are using a floppy disk drive system*).

4. Type **XCOPY C:*.PIC A: /W**

    [If you are using a floppy drive system type **XCOPY A:*.PIC B: /W**]

    The global character (or the wildcard character) can be used with Xcopy just as it was used with the Copy command. The additional switch provided by the /W at the end of the command will allow floppy disk system users to utilize the command. The /W switch makes the system pause before it begins to copy files (if it would not pause, users of floppy drive systems would copy the DOS files because the DOS disk must be in drive A to activate this external command).

5. Press **<CR>**

    The system will pause and prompt you to "press a key to begin copying file(s)".

    If you are using a hard disk system, you are ready and can press the appropriate key to begin the copying process.

    [If you are using a floppy drive system, REMOVE THE DOS DISK from drive A and INSERT the **Understanding and Using MS-DOS/PC DOS** *training disk into drive A. Then press the appropriate key to continue.]*

    The system will first read a copy of each of the files from the source disk and then access the target disk and copy all the files onto it. You should notice that this method of copying is faster than the Copy command because it only needs to access the source disk once. When you use the Copy command, DOS must access the source disk to get a copy of one file and then write the copy to the target disk and then must go back to the source disk to get the next file to copy. Xcopy takes all the files it can possibly hold while it is at the source disk and then writes them all at the same time to the target.

6. Do a directory of your data disk. DIR B: enter

    You should only have the six files with the .PIC extension and the COMMAND.COM file.

7. End of this guided activity. Continue on to the next section.

BACKGROUND ON FORMATTING A DISK WITH A VOLUME LABEL

Since a disk formatted with the system has less room for data files, you will now format your disk without the system. This time, however, you will include a volume label. By using the /V switch with the Format command you are able to put an electronic label (11 characters or less) on your disk.

When you use the DIR or CHKDSK commands, this electronic volume label will be displayed. Remember that the Format command is an external command.

GUIDED ACTIVITY: FORMAT DISK WITH VOLUME LABEL

1. Make sure that DOS is loaded and that the system prompt is displayed.

2. If you are using a hard disk system, the DOS command program files must be available.

    [If you are using a floppy drive system the DOS disk must be in drive A.]

3. Your data disk should be in the data drive (drive A for hard disk systems and *drive B if you are using a floppy disk drive system--remember, floppy users, the DOS disk must be in drive A for this external command*).

4. Type **FORMAT A: /V**

    *[If you are using a floppy drive system type **FORMAT B: /V**]*

5. Press **<CR>**

    When the system prompts you to insert a new disk in the designated drive, make sure that the disk you wish to format is in that designated drive. Depending on which version of DOS you are using, the system will either prompt you to "strike a key to continue" or to press the "RETURN".

6. Press the appropriate key to begin the formatting process.

    A message may appear on the screen indicating that the system is "Formatting..." or providing a head and cylinder count and the in-use light on the designated drive will be on.

7. Part of the process will be completed when a message similar to the one illustrated in Figure 6-5 appears.

Format Complete

Enter desired volume label (11 characters, RETURN for none)?

Figure 6-5, System Requesting Volume Label

8. Type in the label you want to use.

    For example, you might want to use your last name, or your social security number, or assign the disk a number.

9. Press **<CR>**

    When the formatting process is complete, you will be asked if you wish to format another disk. If you wish to format another disk, type the letter "Y" for "yes" and follow the screen prompts to insert a blank disk. If you do not wish to format another disk, type the letter "N" for "no."

10. Type **N** and then press **<CR>**

Your data disk is now ready to be used.

11. Display a wide directory of your data disk.   DIR B: /W

The first line of the directory should now display your volume label and since you have erased your disk, you should receive a "File not found" message. Remember, that indicates that the disk is formatted but does not contain any files.

12. Last guided activity in this unit.

REVIEW QUESTIONS

1. You have decided to change the name of a file that is now named **Branch1.wk1** to **District.1** . The file is stored on the disk that is now in drive B. DOS is loaded and the A> is on the screen. Write the correct command.

   Ren B: Branch 1. wk1 District. 1 ↵

2. The file named **Dispensa.ble** is no longer needed. It is stored on the disk that is in drive A. DOS is loaded and the C> is on the screen. Write the command that will delete the file.

   Del A: Dispensa. ble ↵

3. You are working on a system and are unsure of how much memory is installed. What command can you use to check on the status of the memory? You are using a two-drive floppy disk drive system. Indicate what disk(s) are required, what drive(s) are used for the disk, which program must be loaded, and the other information you may ascertain from the same command that you use to check how much memory is in a system. Your answer should first provide all the requested information and then the command written exactly as you would type it.

   A> CHKDSK ∧ B: ↵   A [DOS]
                           B [file]

4. There is a file on the disk in drive B named **Guess.who**. You don't remember what the file contains. Which DOS command will try to display the data stored in the file on the screen. Write the command exactly as it should be <u>typed</u>. You may assume that DOS is loaded and that the A> is on the screen.

   A> Type B: Guess.who

5. What will the results of this command be?   **FORMAT B: /S/V**

   format the disk in drive B with the system and include a volume label.

6. You've opened a box of new disks and decide to format all the disks at one time. You want to develop a numbering system for the disks and choose to do that through the volume option available in DOS. You may assume that DOS is loaded and that the DOS disk is in drive A. Write the command that will give you the desired results. Is there a way that you can format the entire box of disks without have to retype the command? Explain.

A> Format B: /V

DOCUMENTATION RESEARCH

Subdirectories provide an invaluable tool for organizing your storage disk(s). They can be used on floppies but are absolutely essential on a hard disk. DOS commands allow you to use subdirectories effectively. Use your DOS documentation to find out how it explains the answers to these questions.

1. What is a "multilevel" or "hierarchical directory" system?

2. What is a "path"?

3. How is it possible to have a file with the same name on the same disk?

4. What would this command do? **DIR ..\..**

5. How do you know that a name on a directory listing is a filename and not the name of a subdirectory?

6. How can you rename a directory?

NOTES:

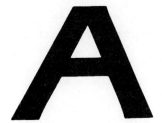

APPLICATION

PRACTICING DOS FILE AND DISK MANAGEMENT COMMANDS

SUPPLIES NEEDED

In order to complete this application section you will need:

1.   this book;
2.   DOS command program files;
3.   the **Understanding and Using MS-DOS/PC DOS** training disk (or files)
4.   data disk.

BACKGROUND ON APPLICATION A

This Application section provides the opportunity to practice the procedures presented thus far in this book including:

1.   following correct start-up and shut-down procedures for using a software program;
2.   following correct procedures for using a printer;
3.   following written instructions regarding microcomputer procedures;
4.   using appropriate DOS commands to accomplish designated tasks;
5.   using the **Understanding and Using MS-DOS/PC DOS** book as a reference to assist you while using the microcomputer.

In this application section you will be given instructions to complete designated tasks, however, the instructions will not be presented in a step-by-step fashion. You will simply be told what must be done and then it is up to you to decide the best procedures to use in order to accomplish the assigned tasks.

You are encouraged to use the previous units in this book as a reference whenever you are in doubt about what should be done. This book will provide a refresher whenever you need to use the DOS commands for disk or file management.

Part 1

1. Use the correct start-up procedures to load the **Understanding and Using MS-DOS/PC DOS** training disk program (you will not need your data disk for this part of the activity).

2. When the **Understanding and Using MS-DOS/PC DOS** Main Menu is on the screen, select "Computer Configuration" and follow the screen prompts that will appear on the screen.

3. When the completed "COMPUTER CONFIGURATION" screen is displayed, print a copy of the screen.

4. Follow correct procedures to advance the paper in the printer. Tear off the paper and put your name and "Application A--Part 1" in the upper right corner of the paper to identify this activity for your instructor.

5. Follow the screen prompts to return to the Main Menu and then exit the program.

Part 2

1. Load DOS. Your data disk should be in the data drive. (Drive A if you are using a hard disk system; *drive B if you are using a floppy system.*)

2. Activate the output to printer so that everything that you do from this step on will appear both on the screen and print on paper. The printed copy must be turned in to your instructor so this step is very important. Remember, we encourage you to use the information in this book as a reference while you are completing this application section.

    (Note: If you are sharing a printer with other workstations, it may be a good idea to print screens at appropriate places rather than tie up the printer for the entire time you are working on this application. For example, after finishing two or three steps, print the screen. Or, if one step fills the screen, print it before going on to the next step.)

3. Format your data disk using the volume label option. When you are prompted to enter the label, enter your first initial and last name (no spaces and no periods).

4. When asked if you want to format another disk, answer "no."

5. Display a full directory of your data disk.

6. If you are using a hard disk system, make sure that the files from the **Understanding and Using MS-DOS/PC DOS** training disk are available.

    [*If you are using a floppy drive system, remove the DOS disk from drive A. Insert the* **Understanding and Using MS-DOS/PC DOS** *training disk in drive A--DO NOT LOAD the program.*]

    Regardless of the type of system you are using, you will be using the data from the **Understanding and Using MS-DOS/PC DOS** training disk to practice some disk and file management. We will refer to this disk as the "training disk" from now on.

7. Display a WIDE directory of the training disk files.

8. Copy the **CALENDAR.BAS** file to your data disk.

9. Display a full directory of your data disk.

10. Copy all the files from the training disk that have a **.BAS** extension to your data disk. Make the copy using just one command.

11. Copy all the files from the training disk that have an **AUTOEXEC** filename. Any extension is acceptable. Make the copy using just one command.

12. Display a wide directory of your data disk.

13. Rename the **SQUARE.BAS** file on **your data disk** to **CIRCLE.BAS**.

14. Display a wide directory of your data disk.

15. If you are using version 3.2 or later, copy all the files from the training disk to your data disk using the XCOPY command otherwise use the COPY command.

16. Display a directory of your data disk that will pause until you indicate that the scrolling should continue. Why is there one more file on your disk than there is on the source disk (the training disk). Write your explanation on the printout of this directory.

17. Use the Type command to display the data stored in the **DOCUMENT.FIL** file that is on your data disk.

18. Delete the **MELLOW.BAS** file from **your data disk**.

19. Display a directory of your data disk that lists only files beginning with the letter "M". You don't care what else is in the filename or its extension.

20. Display a directory of you data disk asking for only the files that have .WK1 as an extension.

21. Delete all the files that have a **.WK1** extension from your data disk.

22. Display a directory of your data disk asking for only the files that have .WK1 as an extension.

23. Check your data disk using the Checkdisk command. (Hint for floppy users: This is an external command.)

24. Format your data disk. Specify your name as the volume label.

25. Display a full directory of your data disk.

26. If you were using output to printer rather than printing the screens, deactivate the output to printer function. Use the correct procedures to advance the paper and put your name and "Application A--Part 2" in the upper right corner of the paper.

27.   Identify each of the steps on your paper with the numbers from each of the steps in Part 2.

28.   Follow the correct shut-down procedures.

NOTES:

UNIT
7 WORKING WITH SUBDIRECTORIES

SUPPLIES NEEDED

In order to complete this unit you will need:

1. this book;
2. DOS command program files;
3. the **Understanding and Using MS-DOS/PC DOS** training disk files;
4. your data disk.

OBJECTIVES

After completing this unit you will be able to:

1. create a subdirectory;
2. change directories;
3. copy files into a specific subdirectory;
4. display a file listing for a specific subdirectory;
5. use the TREE command;
6. remove directories.

IMPORTANT KEYSTROKES AND COMMANDS

MD (MKDIR) .... Create a new subdirectory
RD (RMDIR) .... Remove a subdirectory (must be empty before removed)
CD (CHDIR) .... Change the current directory
TREE .... Display path of each directory and subdirectory
TREE d: /f >prn .... Print path of each directory and their filenames

ASSIGNMENTS

1. _____ Printed Tree (7-1)
2. _____ Printed Directory of data disk (7-2)
3. _____ Printed Tree including filenames (7-3)
4. _____ Printed screens as assigned (7-4 through 7-11)

THE PATH TO ORGANIZATION

Up to this point you have been using just one storage area on your data disk. When you are using a floppy disk, this procedure does not present a problem. However, if you are working on a microcomputer for a business or other type of organization, it is likely that you will be using a hard disk system for both the program files and the data files. Organizing several program files and multiple data files can become extremely difficult if not approached systematically.

Picture if you will an office with just one large room (it only sounds as if your are about to enter the twilight zone). There are three employees working in this one-room office and they all have files of information that they must maintain. They store these files in one huge box in the middle of the room. Whenever they need information from their files, they must rummage through not only their files but also those of their coworkers. One day while looking for a client's file, Ms. Orie Nize came up with a brilliant idea. "Let's set up a filing system. We'll buy a file cabinet for each of us and then label our drawers for the different types of work that we handle." Her coworkers were skeptical but decided it was worth a try. They bought a file cabinet for each person working in the office. Ms. Nize labeled her file cabinet O. Nize (not terribly creative but definitely clear). Mr. Byrd labeled his cabinet B. Byrd and Ms. Numbers labeled hers M. Numbers.

It should go without saying that efficiency really picked up with the implementation of the file cabinet system. The employees organized their work in their own file cabinet. Each drawer in each cabinet was given a name to identify the different tasks handled by each of them. Ms. Nize labeled hers "Correspondence", "Contracts", and "Clients". Now, whenever she needs information about one of her clients she goes to the file cabinet with her name on it and opens the drawer named "Clients". The only files she has to look through are those that fit into that category. If she needs information about one of Mr. Byrd's clients, she simply goes to the file cabinet with his name on it and opens the drawer that he named "Customers". The system worked so well that the company flourished. Ms. Nize was named the efficiency expert for the firm and eventually started her own consulting business.

You too can enjoy a similar success story (or at least be able to use the microcomputer more successfully) if you'll just take a little time now to learn how to organize files into directories and subdirectories on a disk. The concept is the same one used by Ms. Orie Nize. Rather than dumping all your files into one directory on the disk, set up separate named directories in order to increase efficiency.

BACKGROUND ON DIRECTORIES AND SUBDIRECTORIES

When you format a floppy disk or similarly set up a hard disk, there is just one directory created. This main directory is called the **root** directory. It contains the names and other pertinent information about the files stored on the disk. If the disk you are using happens to be a hard disk, your disk has the room to store a lot of files. Trying to find the files you need will become difficult as the list of filenames grows. Another thing to note is that DOS limits the number of files that can be stored in the root directory of a hard disk to

512. Even if the disk still has space available, the space cannot be used if the file limit is reached. By creating subdirectories, you can circumvent this limitation. The only limit will then be the disk's capacity.

A **subdirectory** is a special type of file containing the same type of file directory information that you would find in the root. It will only include the directory information about files that are stored in the subdirectory. This will make it easier for you to work with the files since you will store related files together in subdirectories. When you do a directory of the root, you will only see the names of the files actually stored in the root along with the names of any subdirectories.

A subdirectory can reside in the root directory or in another subdirectory. Subdirectories can be nested -- one pointing to another. You can create additional directories (and subdirectories) in order to work with your files more efficiently. For example, you could set up subdirectories for the data files created with your word processor, and subdirectories for worksheet data files, and still other subdirectories for your database data files Figure 7-1.

You may put your word processing program files in a subdirectory of the root directory. Then you could set up one or more subdirectories of the word processing program directory for data files. If more than one person uses the microcomputer, it would be efficient for each individual to establish their own subdirectories. You could organize your database program and data files in the same way.

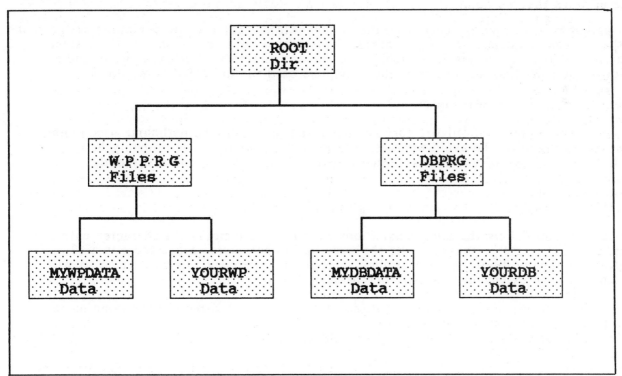

Figure 7-1, Multilevel Directory System

Pathnames

Now that you are beginning to understand the advantages of organizing your files into directories and subdirectories, you must learn how to tell DOS where to find all your well-organized files. In order to do so, you will have to tell DOS what **path** to follow in order to locate the files you want to use. DOS uses **paths** to move from one directory to another. A **pathname** is the sequence of directory names separated by backslashes and ending with the name of the file you wish to use. Just as you would give a person directions to your house by telling her which streets to take, you tell DOS which paths to follow to your files.

As an example, let's say that you create a directory named WPPRG for your word processing program files. Since you share the computer with someone else in the office, you decide to create two subdirectories for data files. One for your documents and one for the other person's documents. Your subdirectory will be named MYWPDATA and the other subdirectory will be named YOURWP.

You have a memo called MEMO1 stored in the MYWPDATA subdirectory. The **pathname** you use to tell DOS where to find that file is:

   \wpprg\mywpdata\memo1

The first backslash tells the system to start at the root directory. Then the path says, "DOS, go into the WPPRG directory and once you are in that directory you'll find another directory called MYWPDATA. Once you are in that directory, you'll find the file named MEMO1."

If a pathname starts with a backslash, the system searches for the file beginning at the root of the directory system. If the pathname begins with a subdirectory name, the system assumes that it should begin its search in the current directory. For example, if you are already in the WPPRG subdirectory, the **pathname** used to find MEMO1 would be:

   mywpdata\memo1

The maximum number of subdirectories is not fixed, however, the pathname used cannot exceed 63 characters. To avoid unnecessary complexity, though, it is probably best to limit subdirectories to one or two levels. Performance will suffer with too many paths.

Directory Names

Directory names follow the same conventions used for filenames -- 1-8 character with an optional 1-3 character extension using the same valid characters. Since there is a 63 character pathname limit, you will probably keep your directory names short. You will seldom assign an extension to a directory name.

Each subdirectory must have a unique name. Do not assign a directory the same name as one of the filenames stored on the disk.

✔ CHECKPOINT

a.   Your colleague has saved a file in the YOURWP subdirectory shown in Figure 7-1. The file is named MEMO2. What pathname would be used to find the file beginning at the root directory?

b.   Using the above example for your colleague, assume that he is working in the WPPRG directory. What pathname would be used to find the MEMO2 file?

_____

BACKGROUND ON MKDIR COMMAND

The MKDIR (make directory) command is an internal command that allows you to create subdirectories. The directories created with this command will become subdirectories of the current directory (sometimes referred to as the working directory) unless you specify otherwise by using a pathname.

A shorter form of the command is MD. We will use the MD version of the command in the guided activities that follow.

Once again we are going to assume that you are either:

using a hard disk system and that drive C is normally the default drive containing the DOS files and the files from the **Understanding and Using MS-DOS/PC DOS** training disk. Drive A will be used for your data disk.

or:

using a two-drive system and that Drive A contains the DOS disk until the files from the **Understanding and using MS-DOS/PC DOS** training disk are needed. Drive B should contain your data disk.

GUIDED ACTIVITY: MAKE SUBDIRECTORIES FOR THE ROOT

1.   Before you begin this guided activity, check to be sure that:

a.   DOS is loaded (the system prompt should be on the screen -- **C:>** if you are using a hard disk system or *A:> if you are using a two-drive floppy system*);

b.   your data disk is blank and formatted (if you use the DIR command you should get the "File not found" message);

c.   your data disk is in the appropriate drive (drive A for most hard disk systems, and *drive B for most floppy systems*).

When you are certain that the above steps have been completed, you will be ready to make a subdirectory named WPPRG (exciting, isn't it). First you will change the default drive.

2.   Type A: [*or B: if you are using a floppy system*]

You want the drive containing your data disk to be the default drive. If your data disk is in a drive other than drive A or B, be sure to type the appropriate letter followed by a colon.

3.   Press **<CR>**

The DOS prompt should reflect the new default drive. Since the MKDIR command is an internal command, you do not have to have the files from the DOS program disk readily available. You are going to create the subdirectories on your data disk rather than on the hard disk, however, the procedure you use on the hard disk is the same as the one you will practice now. You are going to create the subdirectory WPPRG.

4.   Type **MD WPPRG**

5.   Press **<CR>**

Nothing appears to have happened and the system prompt is back on the screen. You will now list a directory of your data disk on the screen. Since your data disk is in the default drive, you only have to use the DIR command...no drive specification is needed.

6.   Type **DIR** then press **<CR>** and the resulting directory should be similar to this:

```
Volume in drive d is YOURNAME
Directory of d:\

WPPRG <DIR>          1-01-90          11:28a
```

The <DIR> in the second column indicates that the name in the first column is a subdirectory name rather than a filename. The date and time that the directory was created appears as the third and fourth columns. You will now create another subdirectory for the root directory.

7.   Type **MD DBPRG**

8.   Press **<CR>**

Again nothing much appears to happen but you have created another subdirectory for the root directory. Display a directory listing.

9.   Type **DIR** then press **<CR>** and the resulting directory should be similar to this:

```
Volume in drive d is YOURNAME
Directory of d:\

WPPRG <DIR>          1-01-90  11:28a
DBPRG <DIR>          1-01-90  11:30a
```

10. Print the screen and label the printout as **Task 7-1**. End of this guided activity. Continue on to the next section.

BACKGROUND ON CREATING A SUBDIRECTORY FOR A SUBDIRECTORY

You have created two subdirectories for the root directory. It is now possible to store files in the root directory or in the WPPRG directory or in the DBPRG directory. If you had done this on a hard disk, you could now copy your word processing program files into the WPPRG directory and your database management system program files into the DBPRG directory. You would have a good start to an organized hard disk.

Let's assume that you want a separate storage area for your word processing documents and database files. A logical approach to organizing these files would be to make a subdirectory in the WPPRG directory for your word processing data files and another subdirectory in the

DBPRG directory for your database data files. As mentioned earlier, the MKDIR command will create a directory for the current directory unless a specific path is given as part of the command.

There are a couple of methods that you can use to create the subdirectories you need. One method will use the full pathname as part of the MKDIR command and the other method will use the CHDIR (change directory) command to change the directory to a different path before using the MKDIR command.

GUIDED ACTIVITY: MAKE A SUBDIRECTORY USING COMPLETE PATHNAME

1. DOS should still be loaded. The default drive (drive A if you are using a hard disk system and *drive B if you are using a floppy system*) should contain your data disk. You are going to make a subdirectory for the WPPRG directory. You are going to name the subdirectory MYWPDATA.

2. Type **MD \WPPRG\MYWPDATA**

   MD is the command. The first backslash tells DOS to start the path at the root directory (be sure that you use backslash, <u>not</u> the forward slash with this command otherwise you will get an error message). The **WPPRG** is the subdirectory of the root and the place where you want to create the subdirectory named **MYWPDATA**. The backslash between **WPPRG** and **MYWPDATA** is necessary to separate the subdirectory names in the pathname.

3. Press **<CR>**

   You have now created a subdirectory for WPPRG.

4. Type **DIR** and then press **<CR>**

   There's no sign of your subdirectory MYWPDATA. What happened? You are still in the root directory. The subdirectory you created was for the WPPRG directory. In order to see a listing with that directory name, you will have to include the complete pathname.

5. Type **DIR \WPPRG** then press **<CR>** and the resulting directory should be similar to this:

   ```
   Volume in drive d is LASTNAME
   Directory of d:\WPPRG

   .              <DIR>        1-01-90  11:45a
   ..             <DIR>        1-01-90  11:45a
   MYWPDATA       <DIR>        1-01-90  11:45a
          3 File(s) 291840 bytes free
   ```

   The single and double dots that you see listed in this directory stand for the current directory and the parent directory. (Every directory except the root directory has a parent.) The single dot is a type of shorthand for the current directory and the double dots are shorthand for the current directory's parent. You'll work with these in an upcoming guided activity (something to look forward to).

6. Print the screen and label the printout as **Task 7-2**. End of this guided activity. Continue on to the next section.

BACKGROUND ON CHANGE DIRECTORY

As we mentioned earlier, the CHDIR command can be used to change the current directory to a different path. It is an internal command and can be abbreviated to CD. We will use the abbreviated version of the command in the guided activities that follow. When you use the CHDIR command to change paths, it is very much like changing the default drive. Now, in addition to default drives, you will also have to consider what the default directory is or should be.

If you are going to do a lot of work in a certain subdirectory, it is a good idea to use the CHDIR command to make it the default directory so it won't be necessary to use the full pathname in commands. For example, when you issued the DIR command in the previous guided activity, you had to specify the complete pathname in order to see the results of your latest creation, the MYWPDATA subdirectory of the WPPRG directory. If you had used the CHDIR command first to make WPPRG the default directory, you could have just typed the DIR command and you would have seen a directory listing that included WPPRG.

In the next guided activity, you will make another subdirectory. This time it will be a subdirectory of the DBPRG directory. You will first use the CHDIR command to change the path so that the current directory is DBPRG and then you will use the MKDIR command to create a subdirectory for DBPRG.

GUIDED ACTIVITY: CHANGE DIRECTORY THEN MAKE DIRECTORY

1. DOS should still be loaded. The default drive should contain your data disk. You are going to make a subdirectory for the DBPRG directory. First you are going to change the directory to DBPRG.

2. Type **CD \DBPRG**

    This tells DOS that you want to change the current directory from the root to the DBPRG directory. (Placing the backslash at the beginning of the pathname tells DOS to start at the root and move to the specified subdirectory.)

3. Press **<CR>**

    Nothing appears to change. However, you do have two methods that you could use to check the current directory. One method is to display a directory listing using the DIR command. This listing does include the complete pathname and any files that may be stored in the current directory. The other method is to use the CD command all by itself to check to see what the current directory is. We'll try that method now.

4. Type **CD** then press **<CR>** and a message similar to the following should appear:

    A:\DBPRG   *[if you are using a floppy system* B:\DBPRG *]*

    This lets you know that the current directory is DBPRG. This is just where you want to be so that you can create a subdirectory for DBPRG.

5. Type **MD MYDBDATA**

    This tells DOS that you want to create a subdirectory for the current directory and you want to name the subdirectory MYDBDATA.

6. Press **<CR>**.

7. Type **DIR** then press **<CR>** and a directory listing similar to the following should
   appear:

   ```
   Volume in drive d is LASTNAME
   Directory of d:\DBPRG

   .               <DIR>        1-01-90  11:50a
   ..              <DIR>        1-01-90  11:50a
   MYDBDATA        <DIR>        1-01-90  11:50a
          3 File(s) 291840 bytes free
   ```

8. Print a copy of the screen and label the printout **TASK 7-3**. End of this guided
   activity. Continue on to the next section.

GUIDED ACTIVITY: MOVING AROUND YOUR SUBDIRECTORIES

1. You should still be in the DBPRG subdirectory. From here you will practice using the
   CHDIR command to move from one directory to another. Hang on, here we go.

2. Type **CD MYDBDATA** then press **<CR>**.

   This tells DOS to move from the current directory, DBPRG, to the subdirectory
   MYDBDATA.

3. Type **CD** then press **<CR>**

   The response should be: d:\DBPRG\MYDBDATA

4. Type **DIR** then press **<CR>** and the screen should look something like this:

   ```
   Volume in drive d is LASTNAME
   Directory of d:\DBPRG\MYDBDATA

   .               <DIR>        1-01-90  11:50a
   ..              <DIR>        1-01-90  11:50a
          2 File(s) 291840 bytes free
   ```

   There are those cute little dots again. Let's try them with a command.

5. Type **DIR ..**   then press **<CR>** and you should get a directory of MYDBDATA's
          parent -- DBPRG.

   ```
   Volume in drive d is LASTNAME
   Directory of d:\DBPRG

   .               <DIR>        1-01-90  11:50a
   ..              <DIR>        1-01-90  11:50a
   MYDBDATA        <DIR>        1-01-90  11:50a
          3 File(s) 291840 bytes free
   ```

   You now want to change the directory to a different path. This time you want to go to
   the parent of the current directory (that would be DBPRG). Rather than typing CD
   \DBPRG, you use the shorthand .. to indicate that you want to move to the parent.

6. Type **CD ..**   then press **<CR>**

7. Type **CD**   then press **<CR>**

    This will check to see that the current directory is now DBPRG. Now we want to change the directory to WPPRG. This is a subdirectory of the root so the pathname will have to begin with the backslash.

8. Type **CD \WPPRG**

    By beginning the pathname with a backslash you are telling DOS that this path begins at the root. Without the backslash, DOS would assume that it could find the WPPRG directory as a subdirectory of the current directory. Since WPPRG is not a subdirectory of DBPRG, which is the current directory, DOS and you would become quite frustrated.

9. Press **<CR>**

10. Type **DIR** then press **<CR>** and a directory listing similar to the following should appear:

    ```
    Volume in drive d is LASTNAME
    Directory of d:\WPPRG

    .              <DIR>          1-01-90   11:50a
    ..             <DIR>          1-01-90   11:50a
    MYWPDATA       <DIR>          1-01-90   11:50a
              3 File(s) 291840 bytes free
    ```

    You want to move into the subdirectory MYWPDATA.

11. Type **CD MYWPDATA**

    You are moving into a subdirectory of the current directory.

12. Press **<CR>**

13. Type **CD** then press **<CR>** to check the current directory.

    The response should be similar to d:\WPPRG\MYWPDATA

    You now want to return directly to the root directory.

14. Type **CD**

    This tells DOS that you want to go directly to the root -- nonstop.

15. Press **<CR>**

16. Type **CD** and then press **<CR>** to check the current directory.

    The response should similar to A:\ (Wasn't that an exciting trip?)

17. End of this guided activity. Continue on to the next section.

UNGUIDED ACTIVITY: CREATE TWO SUBDIRECTORIES ON YOUR OWN

1. Create a subdirectory for WPPRG. Name it YOURWP.

2. Create a subdirectory for DBPRG. Name it YOURDB.

3. Display a directory listing for WPPRG and then one for DBPRG. When both directory listings are on the screen, print the screen. Label the printout **TASK 7-4**.

BACKGROUND ON THE TREE COMMAND

The TREE command will make your trips around your subdirectories much easier because it will provide something like a road map. The TREE command is an external command that provides a screen listing or a hard copy of all the directories and subdirectories on a disk. This is sometimes referred to as a **tree structure directory**.

The TREE command can also include the names of any files stored in each of the directories and subdirectories. Since you don't have any files stored in your directories right now, you'll only print out a tree that includes directory and subdirectory names. In a later guided activity you'll generate a tree that includes filenames (more anticipation!).

GUIDED ACTIVITY: USE THE TREE COMMAND ON YOUR DATA DISK

1. DOS must be loaded and since you are about to use an external command, the DOS command program files must be available. If you are using a hard disk system, the files are probably readily available with no additional preparation (DOS has been told where to find these external command files on the hard disk).

   [*If you are using a two-drive floppy system, make sure that the DOS disk is in drive A before you issue the TREE command.*]

   Your disk should be in the data drive. The data drive can still be the default drive.

2. Be sure that the printer connected to your system is online.

3. If you are using a hard-drive system type **C:TREE A: >PRN**

   [*If you are using a two-drive floppy system type **A:TREE B: >PRN**]*

   This tells DOS to go to the drive where it will find the DOS command program file for the TREE command. The <space> followed by a drive letter and colon tells DOS which drive contains the disk for which you want the tree structure. Finally, the greater than sign (>) followed by PRN tells DOS to send the results of this command to the printer rather than to the screen.

4. Press **<CR>**

   The listing should print on paper (not on the screen).

5. When the printout is completed, remove it from the printer. Examine the contents of the tree structure. Notice the PATH and SUB-DIRECTORIES for each path are included. The printout should include all the directories and subdirectories that you have created up to this point. Label the printout as **TASK 7-5**.

BACKGROUND ON COPYING FILES INTO SUBDIRECTORIES

You know how to copy files from one disk to another. You use these same commands to copy from one disk to another disk into a specific subdirectory or from one subdirectory to another on the same disk. The only difference will be the inclusion of a pathname as part of the command. If you are going to copy several files into a specific subdirectory, it is a good idea to make that target directory the default. You can include the wildcard and/or global characters whenever needed to copy multiple files to and from subdirectories.

GUIDED ACTIVITY: COPY FILES INTO \DBPRG\MYDBDATA SUBDIRECTORY

1. DOS should still be loaded. You will now need access to the files from the **Understanding and Using MS-DOS/PC DOS** training disk.

   If you are using a hard disk, be sure to follow the necessary procedures so that you can work with files from this disk. (Remember, each lab will have a specific procedure for you to follow in order to get to these files on the hard disk. Now that you have had an introduction to using subdirectories, you may find that you have been using them on the hard disk system in your lab without really understanding what you were doing. Isn't it great to be able to begin putting these microcomputer puzzle pieces together. The files from the **Understanding and Using MS-DOS/PC DOS** training disk are probably stored in a subdirectory on the hard disk. In order to get to them you may have been using the CHDIR command.) **We will caution you now using that age-old adage...*a little bit of knowledge can be a dangerous thing*...be adventurous and/or experimental with your data disk, not with someone else's hard disk.**

   [*If you are using a two-drive floppy system, remove DOS from drive A and insert the* **Understanding and Using MS-DOS/PC DOS** *training disk into drive A.]*

2. The data drive should be the default drive and should still contain your data disk. The the default directory should be the root.

   To be sure that you have access to the necessary files, you will display a directory listing the files on the **Understanding and Using MS-DOS/PC DOS** training disk.

3. If you are using a hard disk system, type **DIR C: /W**

   [*If you are using a two-floppy system, type* **DIR A: /W**]

4. Press **<CR>**

   A wide directory listing the files will appear. (You should be pretty familiar with this file listing by now. If the listing is not the same as it has been for all previous guided activities, go over the steps again to be sure that you have followed the correct procedures so that you can access these files. Then, continue with this guided activity.)

   You are going to copy all the files with the extension .FIL into the MYDBDATA subdirectory of the DBPRG directory.

5. If you are using a hard disk system, type **COPY C:*.FIL   \DBPRG\MYDBDATA**

   [*If using a floppy system type* **COPY A:*.FIL   \DBPRG\MYDBDATA**]

6. Press **<CR>**

The files with an .FIL extension will copy from the source drive to the target drive into the specified MYDBDATA subdirectory. (The path starts at the root -- the beginning backslash -- then goes into the DBPRG subdirectory and from there into the MYDBDATA subdirectory.) You are going to send a directory listing to the printer so that you can see the results of the copy command. Be sure that the printer you are going to use is on-line.

7. Type **DIR \DBPRG\MYDBDATA >PRN** and then press **<CR>**

8. Label the printout as **TASK 7-6**.

9. End of this guided activity. Continue on to the next section.

GUIDED ACTIVITY: COPY FILES INTO \WPPRG\MYWPDATA SUBDIRECTORY

You are going to copy all the files without an extension (this requires using the global character and a period to indicate no extension -- ***.**) into the MYWPDATA subdirectory of the WPPRG directory.

1. If you are using a hard disk system, type **COPY C:*. \WPPRG\MYWPDATA**

    [*If you are using a floppy system type* **COPY A:*. \WPPRG\MYWPDATA**]

2. Press **<CR>**

    You are goint to print a directory of the \WPPRG\MYWPDATA subdirectory.

3. Type **DIR \WPPRG\MYWPDATA >PRN** and then press **<CR>**

    Label the printout as **TASK 7-7**.

4. End of this guided activity. Continue on to the next section.

GUIDED ACTIVITY: COPY FILES INTO \WPPRG SUBDIRECTORY

You are going to copy all the .BAS files into the \WPPRG subdirectory. This time, before copying the files, you are going to change the current directory so the target directory is the default directory.

1. Type **CD \WPPRG**   and then press **<CR>**

2. Type **CD** and then press **<CR>**

    If the current directory is \WPPRG you are ready to continue.

3. If you are using a hard disk system, type **COPY C:*.BAS** and then press **<CR>**

    [*If you are using a floppy system type* **COPY A:*.BAS** *and then press* **<CR>**]

    You do not have specify the target pathname because you took the time to change the current directory so that it is the default. This command tells DOS what source to copy from but does not specify a target. Therefore, DOS will use the default drive and directory as the target.

4. Type **DIR >PRN** and then press **<CR>**

    This will send a copy of the directory to the printer. The directory should only include files with the .BAS extension.

5. Label the printout as **TASK 7-8**.

6. End of this guided activity. Continue on to the next section.

GUIDED ACTIVITY: COPY FILES INTO \WPPRG\YOURWP SUBDIRECTORY

You will change the current directory to \WPPRG\YOURWP before copying all the files that have **COPY** as the filename.

1. Type **CD \WPPRG\YOURWP**   and then press **<CR>**

2. Type **CD** and then press **<CR>**

    If you are in the \WPPRG\YOURWP subdirectory, you are ready to copy all the files with COPY as a filename.

3. If you are using a hard disk system, type **COPY C:COPY.***

    [*If you are using a floppy system type* **COPY A:COPY.***]

4. Press **<CR>**

5. Type **DIR >PRN**   and then press **<CR>**

    This will send a copy of the file list of the subdirectory to the printer. Only COPY filenames should be included in the listing.

6. Label the printout as **TASK 7-9**.

7. End of this guided activity. Continue on to the next section.

BACKGROUND ON REMOVING SUBDIRECTORIES

The RMDIR command (shortened to RD) is used to remove subdirectories from a disk. Before you can use the command, however, all files and any of its subdirectories must be deleted from the directory you plan to eliminate. The subdirectory you want to remove cannot be the current directory.

GUIDED ACTIVITY: REMOVE \DBPRG\YOURDB

You are going to remove the \DBPRG\YOURDB subdirectory. There are no files in that subdirectory so there won't be any problem when you try to remove it. You will remove this subdirectory while the root directory is current.

1. Type **CD ** and then press **<CR>**   This will make the root directory current.

2. Type **RD \DBPRG\YOURDB**   and then press **<CR>**

This tells DOS to remove the subdirectory YOURDB from the directory DBPRG which is a subdirectory of the root. You will now print a directory of the \DBPRG subdirectory.

3. Type **DIR \DBPRG >PRN**   and then press **<CR>**

This will send a copy of the \DBPRG directory to the printer. Notice that the only subdirectory left in the \DBPRG directory is MYDBDATA.

4. Label the printout as **TASK 7-10.**

5. End of this guided activity. Continue on to the next section.

GUIDED ACTIVITY: REMOVE THE \WPPRG\YOURWP SUBDIRECTORY

You are going to attempt to remove a subdirectory that contains files. DOS will send you an error message when you attempt to do this. You will then have to erase the files from the subdirectory and attempt the removal again.

1. Make sure that you are in the root directory. Type **CD ** and then press **<CR>**

2. Type **RD \WPPRG\YOURWP**

3. Press **<CR>**

A message similar to the following will appear: *Invalid path, not directory, or directory not empty*. Obviously, something is wrong. Time to check into the problem.

4. Type **CD \WPPRG\YOURWP**   and then press **<CR>**

This will make the subdirectory that you want to remove, the current directory.

5. Type **DIR *.*** and then press **<CR>**

There they are...the four files that make it impossible for you to remove this subdirectory. (The . **<DIR>** and the .. **<DIR>** will not prevent you from removing the subdirectory. However, files or named subdirectories for the subdirectory you wish to eliminate will prevent its removal.) You will now use the DEL command to erase the files. You can use the DEL *.* command because the command will only erase all the files in the current directory.

6. Type **DEL *.*** and then press **<CR>**

This tells DOS to erase all files from the current directory. A message will ask if you are sure. Since you did do a directory of this subdirectory before issuing the command, you are sure that you want these files erased.

7. Type **Y**   and then press **<CR>**

This indicates that you want to go ahead with the deletion. Now you are ready to remove this directory. You cannot do that while it is still the current directory. We'll move back one level to its parent and then remove it.

8. Type **CD ..**   and then press **<CR>**

9. Type **CD**   and then press **<CR>**

    You should now be in the \WPPRG subdirectory and you are ready to remove one of its subdirectories ... YOURWP.

10. Type **RD YOURWP** and then press **<CR>**

    You do not want to type a backslash before the subdirectory name because it is not a subdirectory of the root. It is a subdirectory of the current directory. You are going print a directory.

11. Type **DIR >PRN**   and then press **<CR>**

    The only subdirectory included in the printed directory should be the MYWPDATA.

12. Label the printout as **TASK 7-11**.

13. End of this guided activity. Continue on to the next section.

GUIDED ACTIVITY: PRINT A TREE WITH FILENAMES

You are going to print a tree structure that includes the filenames for each of the subdirectories. Remember, since TREE is an external command, DOS command files must be available. If you are using a hard disk, the external DOS commands are probably available without any additional work on your part. If you are using a floppy system, you must be sure that the DOS disk is in drive A before you continue.

1. Check to be sure that DOS external commands are available and that the printer is on-line before you continue. Your disk should be in the data drive and the data drive is the default drive.

2. If you are using a hard disk system, type **C:TREE /F >PRN** and then press **<CR>**

    [*If you are using a floppy system, type* **A:TREE /F >PRN** *and then press* **<CR>**]

    (Note: That's a forward slash that you are using to add the "filename" parameter to the TREE command. Don't confuse it with the backslash that you've been using quite a bit in this unit.) A copy of the tree structure for your data disk should print out. It should include each of the directories and the names of the files that are stored in each one.

3. Label the printout **TASK 7-12**.

    You are going to format your disk. Therefore, change the default drive so that it's back to what it was when you started (drive C for most hard disk users and *drive A for most floppy disk system users*).

4. Format your data disk so that it will be ready for the next application.

5. Last guided activity in this book. Good luck with Application B...you're going to love it.

REVIEW QUESTIONS

1. How many characters can be in a pathname?

2. If a pathname starts with a backslash, where will the system look for the first subdirectory listed in the pathname?

3. You have a file named **REPORT** stored in the **WPPRG** subdirectory. You decide you are going to have other reports and you want to set up a subdirectory for them. You are going to name the subdirectory **REPORT**.

   You want to make the **REPORT** directory a subdirectory of **WPPRG** so you are going to type this command to accomplish it: **MD \WPPRG\REPORT**

   Do you see any problems with this plan? If so, what problem(s) can you anticipate? How could you resolve the problem(s) that you see? If there is no problem with the current plan or once you resolve any problem(s) you saw, how will you get the **REPORT** file into the new subdirectory?

4. You have a subdirectory in the root of your hard disk named **BOULDER**. **BOULDER** has a subdirectory named **ROCK**. **ROCK** has a subdirectory named **STONE**. You want to copy a client's file into the **STONE** subdirectory. The name of the file is **Rubble**. Write the command that will allow you to copy the file from a floppy disk that's in drive A to the correct subdirectory on drive C.

5. How would you create a subdirectory for the **STONE** directory described in #3. Assume that you are going to name the subdirectory **PEBBLE**.

6. You want to know what subdirectories are set up on the hard disk you are using. What command will you enter to find out that information? Write the command exactly as you would type it.

7. You want to send the list of the directories, subdirectories, and the filenames stored in each directory to the printer rather than listing the information on the screen. Write the command exactly as you would type it to accomplish that task.

NOTES:

APPLICATION B

PRACTICING DOS FILE AND SUBDIRECTORY COMMANDS

SUPPLIES NEEDED

In order to complete this application section you will need:

1. this book;
2. DOS programs;
3. the **Understanding and Using MS-DOS/PC DOS** training disk (or files)
4. your formatted data disk.

BACKGROUND ON APPLICATION B

This Application section provides the opportunity to practice the procedures presented in this book including:

1. creating subdirectories;
2. changing subdirectories;
3. copying files into subdirectories;
4. using the TREE command;
5. deleting subdirectories.

In this application section you will be given instructions to complete designated tasks, however, the instructions will not be presented in a step-by-step fashion. You will simply be told what must be done and then it is up to you to decide the best procedures to use in order to accomplish the assigned tasks.

You are encouraged to use the previous units in this book as a reference whenever you are in doubt about what should be done.

Part 1 MAKE SUBDIRECTORIES

Check to be sure that you are ready to begin:

1.   DOS should be loaded.

2.   Your blank, formatted data disk should be in the data drive. (Drive A for most hard disk systems or *Drive B for most floppy disk systems.*)

3.   Make the data drive the default drive.

     For example, if your data disk is in drive A then drive A, should be the default drive. *If your data disk is in drive B, then drive B should be the default drive.*

You should now be ready to make subdirectories on your data disk.

Make the following subdirectories:

1.   Create the following directories on your data disk:

     \LOTUS
     \LOTUS\WRKSHEET
     \LOTUS\GRAPHS

     \DBASE
     \DBASE\CUSTOMER
     \DBASE\RENTALS

     \MEMOS
     \LETTERS
     \SPECIAL

2.   Print out a TREE that includes the directory and subdirectory names that are on your data disk. (Remember that TREE is an external command. Be sure to make any adjustments in the defaults you are using.)

3.   Label the printout with your name and "Application B--Part 1" to identify this activity for your instructor.

Part 2 COPY FILES INTO SUBDIRECTORIES

Check to be sure that you are ready to begin:

1.   DOS should be loaded.

2.   Your data disk with the subdirectories created in Part 1 should be in the data drive. (Drive A for most hard disk systems or *Drive B for most floppy disk systems.*)

3.   The files from the **Understanding and Using MS-DOS/PC DOS** training disk should be available.

If you are using a hard disk system, follow the procedures you have been using to make certain that the files from the training disk are available on the hard disk. You will be copying some of these files into subdirectories on your data disk.

If you are using a floppy system, remove the DOS disk from drive A and insert the **Understanding and Using MS-DOS/PC DOS** *training disk into drive A. You will be copying some of the files from the training disk into the subdirectories on your data disk.*

4. Hint: Be sure that the subdirectory you want to copy to is the current directory before you issue the appropriate copy command.

Copy the files:

You should be ready to begin copying files. The source disk will be the **Understanding and Using MS-DOS/PC DOS** training disk files.

1. You want a printout of the copy commands that you use to accomplish each of the copying tasks given in the next step. In order to do this you will either have to activate the output to printer function or remember to print the screen at the appropriate points in your work so that each command and the results will print on paper.

2. Copy these files: To this subdirectory on your data disk:

    (a)

    1AR.WKS   \LOTUS\WRKSHEET
    2AR.WKS
    3AR.WKS
    AR1.WKS
    AR2.WKS
    AR3.WKS

    (b)

    FILE1.PIC   \LOTUS\GRAPHS
    FILE2.PIC
    FILE3.PIC
    AR1.PIC
    AR2.PIC
    AR3.PIC

    (c)

    All files that have   \DBASE\CUSTOMER
    NEWABC as the filename

(continue on next page)

<u>Copy these files:</u>   <u>To this subdirectory on your data disk:</u>

(d)

All files that have   \DBASE\RENTALS
ABC1 as the filename

(e)

BLAIRLIN.DOC   \LETTERS

(f)

LIB.DOC   \SPECIAL
LEASE.KEY

(g)

MEMO1   \MEMOS
MEMO2
MEMO3

3.   Label each part of the printout with the task letters shown in parentheses (x) above each group of files.

4.   <u>Use the TREE command</u> to provide a listing of the tree structure of your data disk. The listing must include filenames for each subdirectory. Output should be directed to the printer. (Remember that TREE is an external command.)

5.   Put your name and "Application B--Part 2" on the printout.

Part 3 REMOVE SUBDIRECTORIES

1.   Be sure that DOS is loaded and that your data disk with the subdirectories and files from Parts 1 and 2 is in the data drive.

2.   Remove the \MEMOS subdirectory.

3.   Remove the \DBASE subdirectory.

4.   Print a TREE with filenames for your data disk.

5.   Put your name and "Application B--Part 3" on the printout.

6.   Format your data disk so that it will be ready for your next adventures with the microcomputer. Happy computing!

APPENDIX

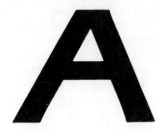

ANSWERS TO CHECKPOINT QUESTIONS

Page 67

8.   one file, PROG.FIL

Page 69

4.   three files, all with .FIL extensions

Page 70

4.   seven files, four with COPY filenames, three with .FIL extensions

Page 70

4.   (end of page) thirteen files, six with "any" one beginning character followed by AR and any extension, four with COPY filenames, three with .FIL extensions

Page 77

a.   DIR *d:*COPY.*

Page 78

b.   The COPY filename is should not be on the directory. Its name was changed to COPY.4; that filename should be listed in the directory.

Page 79

c.   REN *d:*MENU.BAS MENU1.BAS

d.   DIR *d:*MENU*.*

Page 83

e.   An external command is not loaded into the system's memory when you load DOS. The programs for external commands are stored on disk until you execute one of the commands. The system then goes to the disk for the program for the command you entered. If you are using a hard disk system, the system must be set up so that it knows where to find these command programs. If you are using a floppy drive system, the DOS disk must be in the drive. An internal command is loaded into the system's memory at the time when DOS is loaded. The system has access to the program instructions for the internal commands and does not have to access the disk in order to execute these types of commands.

f. through g. Answers will vary somewhat depending upon the system being used.

Page 100

a.   \WPPRG\YOURWP\MEMO2

Page 101

b.   YOURWP\MEMO2

APPENDIX

B

GLOSSARY

Adapter Card printed circuit boards that can be plugged into slots in the motherboard so that you can attach a peripheral, add more memory, or some other function to the microcomputer system.

Applications variety of tasks that can be done on a microcomputer such as word processing, accounting, database management, graphics, project management, desktop publishing, and so on.

Application Program list of instructions that tell the microcomputer how to do the things that a user wants done such as how to be a word processor that will allow the user to type memos, letters, and reports; or how to be a database management system that will keep track of clients, accounts payable, accounts receivable and so on.

Backup additional copy of a file that can be used if a disk is damaged

Bad sectors spots on a floppy disk or a hard disk that have lost their ability to store data

Boot start the microcomputer system. See "Cold boot" and "Warm Boot".

Buffer temporary storage area usually found in peripheral devices such as keyboards, printers, and so on.

Byte the equivalent of one character (8 bits)

Chip a small piece of silicon that is imprinted with microcircuits

Cold boot start a microcomputer system that is turned off by using the power switch to turn it on.

Compatible systems that can read from and write to the same disks

CPU   central processing unit. In a microcomputer system the CPU is a chip approximately 2 1/2" that controls the systems arithmetic and logic operations (sometimes referred to as the ALU ... arithmetic/logic unit). It also contains the control unit that supervises the functioning the the machine as a whole receiving instructions from programs.

CRT   see "Display"

Cursor   a small blinking line or box that indicates where the next character will appear on the screen

Data   information

Default   a specification that will be assumed by a program unless changed by the user. ex. the default drive when using DOS is usually indicated by the system prompt...A> or C>...the commands you execute will assume you mean to do something to the disk in the drive indicated by the system prompt unless you specify the drive as part of the command.

Disk drive   an input/output device that is installed in the system unit or attached to the PC that spins the disk and transfers data to and from the microcomputer system. There can be a hard disk drive and/or floppy disk drive(s) in a system.

Display   output device that produces data visually on a screen; monitor; screen (sometimes even referred to as a CRT...cathode ray tube).

Documentation   instructions that are provided with software programs and hardware telling you what procedures to follow in order to get the software or hardware to perform correctly

DOS   set of system programs that manages microcomputer hardware, software, and stored data. For example, it controls all data input and output; it acts as an interface between application software and the hardware by translating instructions from application software so that the hardware can understand; it checks to be sure that the entire system is functioning properly and provides messages when it is not; and it controls all areas of file management.

DOS prompt   see "System prompt"

File   a collection of data representing a set of entities with certain aspects in common and organized for some specific purpose (an entity is any data object such as certain employee or contract). A file can also be defined as a data structure stored in external memory. A file is also defined as an organized collection of data stored on some external storage device, in other words, a group of related data stored on a disk.

Gigabyte   Over one billion bytes.

Hard disk   (fixed disk) a rigid material with a magnetic coating hermetically sealed in its drive, used to store massive quantities of data

Hardware   the part of the computer system that can be seen and touched; the equipment.

Input   data put into the system

Input device   piece of hardware used to get information into the system such as a keyboard, disk drive, mouse, scanner, and so on.

Keyboard   most frequently-used input device for microcomputers; different 84-key or 101-key configuration will usually include alphabetic, numeric, function, directional arrow, and other special-purpose keys.

Kilobyte   1024 bytes (rounded to 1000).

Logged drive   see "Default"

Main Menu   a list of functions that many software programs provide to make it easier for the user to execute the functions.

Megabyte   1,048,576 bytes (rounded to 1 million bytes).

Memory   device with the capacity to store data so that it can be retrieved when needed

Microcomputer   a small computer containing a central processing unit (CPU), memory for storing data and programs, I/O interfaces for exchanging data with peripherals, and the circuitry to control the flow of data. The physical size of these computers can vary anywhere from laptops to desktops.

Monitor   see "Display"

Output   information coming out of a microcomputer system

Output device   piece of hardware used to get information out of a system such as a printer, disk drive, video display, plotter, and so on

Parameters   variables that can be added to a command or a program

Peripheral   additional hardware devices that can be added to a microcomputer such as printers, displays, keyboards, disk drives, modems.

Pixel   a dot on a video display that is part of the output that is seen

Printer   output device that produces data on paper; generates hard copy. Different types of printers include dot matrix, laser, ink jet and daisy wheel.

Program   see "Software"

Random Access Memory   RAM, eraseable memory located inside of a system used to temporarily store data and allow it to be retrieved as needed

Read from disk   get information from a disk to use immediately or to store in the systems random access memory.

Read-write heads   device inside drive that reads information from a disk and stores information on a disk.

Screen   see "Display"

Scrolling   movement of characters on the screen. Movement may be either vertical (vertical scrolling) where lines move off the top of the screen as new ines appear on the bottom of the screen or horizontal (horizontal scrolling) where in some programs, as characters are typed across the screen, some characters will move off the left or right side in order to show characters on the other side of the screen.

Software   programs (list of instructions) that tell a microcomputer what to do. Some programs are application programs and some are called system programs. (See "application program" and "system program".)

Submenu   a menu that appears as the result of a previous menu selection.

System Program   list of instructions written so that the microcomputer knows how to manage and control the hardware, software, and stored data. DOS is an example of of collection of interrelated system programs.

System Prompt   the system's way of letting you know that it's waiting for you to type information. It also indicates the default drive (ex. A> B> C>)

Terabyte   over one trillion bytes.

Typematic   keys that will repeat when held down

Video display   see "Display"

Warm boot   Restart a microcomputer system that is already turned on. Usually use the Ctrl + Alt + Del key combination or a Reset key to accomplish this.

Write to disk   store data onto a disk.

INDEX

Index

P

Paper, adjust in printer, 53
Path, 100
Pathname, 100
Pause screen function, 40
Peripheral, 2, 5
Pixels, 5
Print, Output to printer, 9, 36, 47-48
Print screen, 36, 45-46
Printer, 2, 6-7, 25, 45-46, 53
Program, 4, 6, 20, 21, 24, 32, 52, 54-55
Prompt, 55-56
    (See "DOS prompt")

R

Random access memory, 4, 12, 81-82
Read to disk, 25
Rename command, 62, 65, 75-78
Rename file, 65, 76, 78
    (See "Rename command", "Copy to rename
    a file")
Resolution, 5-6
RMDIR, 62, 97, 110-112
Root directory, 98-100, 101

S

Scrolling, 40
Self-loading (self-booting), 85
Shut-down procedures, 32-33
Software, (See "Programs")
Sort command, 43, 62
Source disk, 65-67, 88
Start-up procedures, 24
Storage capacity,
    units of measure, 11-12
Subdirectories (See "Directories")
System board (See "Motherboard")
System prompt (See "DOS prompt")
System unit, 2

T

Target disk, 65-67, 88
Time, 28-29, 31, 40
Time command, 31, 62
Toggle keys (See "Keyboard")
Tree command, 62, 97, 107, 112

Tree structure directory, 107
Type command, 62, 76, 84-85
Typematic (See "Keyboard")

U

Update a File, 73

V

Video display, 2, 5-6
        Color, 6
        Monochrome, 6
Volume label, 38, 88-89

W

Warm boot, 24, 26-28
Wildcard character, 67, 70, 79
        (See "Global character")
Write-protect, 15, 43, 61
Write to disk, 25-26

X

Xcopy command, 62, 76, 87-88

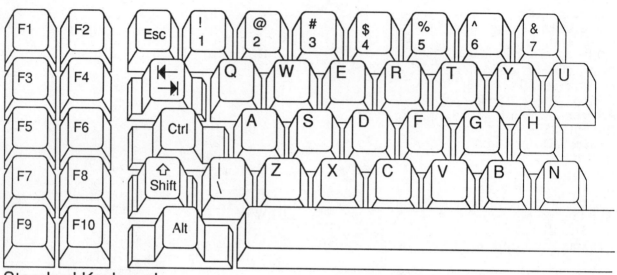

Standard Keyboard

DOS Keyboard

F1   Playback last command, character by character
F2   Playback last command up to a specific character
F3   Playback repeats entire last command
F4   Skip characters in last command up to a specific character
F5   Saves currently displayed line for editing and advances to next line

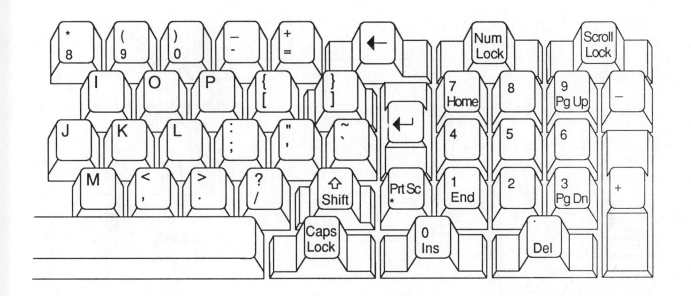

IBM PC™ Abbreviations

Esc—Escape Key   PrtSc—Print Screen Key

Ctrl—Control Key   Pg Dn—Page Down Key

Alt—Alternate Key   Ins—Insert Character

Num Lock—Number Lock Key   Del—Delete Character

Pg Up—Page Up Key

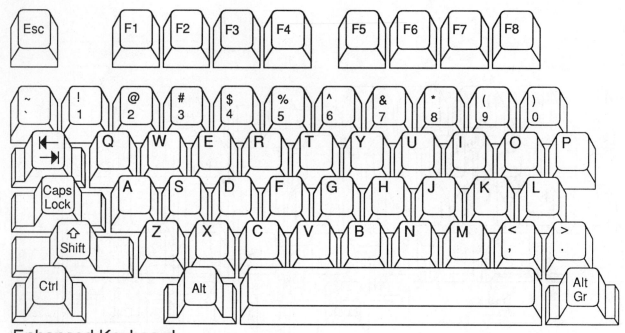

Enhanced Keyboard

DOS Keyboard

F1   Playback last command, character by character
F2   Playback last command up to a specific character
F3   Playback repeats entire last command
F4   Skip characters in last command up to a specific character
F5   Saves currently displayed line for editing and advances to next line

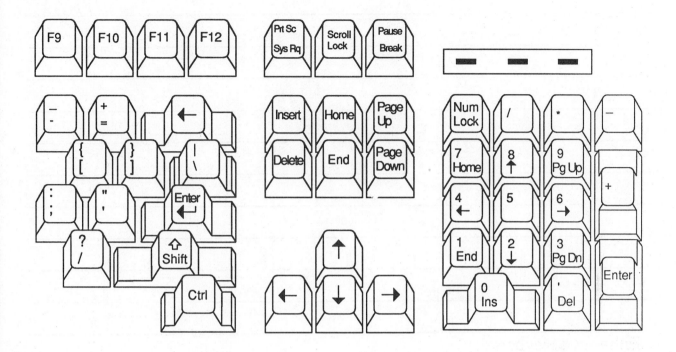

IBM PC™ Abbreviations

Esc—Escape Key   PrtSc—Print Screen Key

Ctrl—Control Key   Pg Dn—Page Down Key

Alt—Alternate Key   Ins—Insert Character

Num Lock—Number Lock Key   Del—Delete Character

Pg Up—Page Up Key

NOTES

NOTES

NOTES

NOTES

NOTES

NOTES

To remove includes a backslash \

Everyelse if forwardslash /

i/P Cpause

h

LOUISE   873-9210

* .pic

. pic
pie
pik

.pie

t/dis
.tgt
ter.

..t?.F

MS-DOS®/PC DOS

```
d - drive/directory       filename - file to use       ext - extension to use
      designation                    in command                    in command

                          ^ - press <space>
```

FUNCTION   COMMAND

```
To check disk in designated drive                    CHKDSK^d:
To clear screen                                       CLS

To copy named file from source to target             COPY^d:filename.ext^d:
To copy files with same filename                      COPY^d:filename.*^d:
To copy files with same extension                     COPY^d:*.ext^d:
To copy all files from source to target              COPY^d:*.*^d:
To copy using wildcard in one position (?)            COPY^d:filen?me.ext^d:
To copy and rename a file (can be same disk)          COPY^d:original.ext^d:newname.ext

To reset system date                                 DATE
To reset system time                                 TIME

To erase named file                                  DEL^d:filename.ext
To erase files with same filename                     DEL^d:filename.*
To erase files with same extension                    DEL^d:*.ext

To display a full directory                          DIR  or  DIR^d:
To display a full directory with a pause             DIR/P or DIR^d:^/P
To display a wide directory                          DIR/W or DIR^d:^/W
To display a sorted directory                        DIR^|SORT or DIR^d:^|SORT

To make an exact copy of disk (erases target)        DISKCOPY^d:^d:

To format a disk in designated drive                 FORMAT^d:
To format designated disk with volume label          FORMAT^d:^/V
To format disk with system                           FORMAT^d:^/S

To rename a file on disk                             REN^d:oldname.ext^newname.ext

To make a new subdirectory                           MD^dirname  (or pathname)
To change named directory to root                    CD^\
To change named directory (starts at root)           CD^\dirname (or pathname)
To remove directory (must be empty)                  RD^\dirname (or pathname)
To list directories and subdirectories               TREE^d:
    ...with filenames                                TREE^d:^/F

To display contents of file                          TYPE^d:filename.ext
To copy designated files with version                XCOPY^d:filename.ext^d:
    3.2 or newer

To boot the system                                   CTRL + ALT + DEL
To activate output to printer                        CTRL + PrtSc key
                                                         or just PrtSc key
To print a copy of the screen                        <SHIFT> + PrtSc key
```